FISHER-PRICE TOYS

A PICTORIAL PRICE GUIDE TO THE MORE POPULAR TOYS

BRAD CASSITY

COLLECTOR BOOKS

A Division of Schroeder Publishing Co., Inc.

Searching For A Publisher?

We are always looking for knowledgeable people considered experts within their fields. If you feel that there is a real need for a book on your collectible subject and have a large comprehensive collection, contact Collector Books.

On The Cover

Top row from left to right:
#766 Sesame Street Lacing Puppets
#8120 My Friend Christy
#370 Trail Boss
#125 Music Box Iron
#741 Teddy Zilo
#136 Lacing Shoe

Cover design: Beth Summers
Book design: Holly C. Long

Collector Books
P.O. Box 3009
Paducah, KY 42002-3009
www.collectorbooks.com

CONTENTS

Acknowledgments

The author and editor/advisor wish to thank the following individuals for their help and encouragement in the preparation of this book: Deanna Korth, Jeanne Kennedy, Bruce Inglis, Ted Furcht, Daniel Leeds, Rose Perine, Michelle Kopp, Dani Crissman, and an anonymous friend. A very special thank you to the following folks at Blue Ribbon for their guidance, help, and work: Gesina Bernstein, Richard Rodriguez, and Stephanie Harkless. We also thank our wives, Myrna Combs and Gloria Cassity, and Brad's children, Jenna, Dinah, and Christina Cassity, for their understanding and help in the preparation of this book. I would also like to thank Jen Mickle, Allen and Louise Cassity, Len Athanasiades, and Lisa Bagley.

I would like to thank those people who have been an instrumental part of my life. Without them I would not be where I am today. First, my family who have been most supportive of this project. My brother Beau and his wife Loni, Jeanne Kennedy, and Deanna Korth who have never-ending hearts. They are more than just friends, but a part of my family. I will always have a special place in my heart for them.

Brad A. Cassity, Photography, Historical Research/Word Processing
Gary Combs, Editor/Advisor

Toys And Society

In the largest sense, toys can be a social force used to shape and mold our children into the kind of human beings we hope they will be in the future. Toys also reflect the nature of our society. They reflect our concerns and preoccupations as a people and a nation; they reflect our expectations and our aspirations. They frequently tell us more about ourselves than they tell our children about themselves.

About The Author

BRAD CASSITY was born, raised, and educated in Silver Spring, Maryland, and is presently residing in Toledo, Ohio. An avid collector of Fisher-Price toys for many years, he is an advisor on Fisher-Price toys to *Schroeder's Collectible Toys, Antique to Modern-Price Guide,* and *Toy Shop,* one of the largest monthly toy magazines. He was instrumental in establishing the Fisher-Price file on the America On-Line Toy Board, restoring and transferring TV commercials by Fisher-Price on 8mm film strip to video tapes, and is an ardent supporter of the Fisher-Price Collectors Club, the Toy Town USA Museum, and the ToyFest Festival. Brad began collecting Fisher-Price toys after receiving advice from his brother Beau, seriously collecting and researching Fisher-Price toys after his first visit to ToyFest in 1993 and meeting his mentors Deanna Korth, Jeanne Kennedy, and Stirling Muck.

Editor/Advisor
GARY P. COMBS DVM, MPH, is a retired U.S. Department of Agriculture Veterinarian who has been collecting and researching Fisher-Price toys for over six years. While in the U.S. Department of Agriculture, Dr. Combs was assigned duty in Australia, Great Britain, Dominican Republic, and Puerto Rico. He and his family spent six years in Puerto Rico after which he returned to the United States. He retired from the USDA in 1991. Now he collects and researches Fisher-Price toys.

INTRODUCTION

In 1985 a pictorial book about toys was published. It used to be the book to use as a reference in the world of Fisher-Price Toys. In 1987, a new book was published and it strictly engaged all Fisher-Price Toys from 1931 – 1963. While each of these books is a great asset in terms of collecting, more references are constantly needed and the demand here is very great. This book was developed to include the many toys that were discussed in the previously written books.

The intention of this book is to cover toys produced from 1964 – 1990. This includes pull (or push) toys, musical toys, puzzles, dolls, the famous Play Family and Little People Playsets, Adventure series toys, Husky Helpers and vehicles, ToyFest Limited Editions and memorabilia, Movie Viewers and cartridges, and a miscellaneous section covering toys not made by Fisher-Price but bearing their name. Occasionally a picture is not shown. At press time one may not have been available and it is indicated by an N/A.

This book was written to provide the most in-depth information to the collector we had at the time of publication. We hope one will never have to guess what goes where because it will be contained within this book with as much accuracy as the research and materials on hand could provide. It is hoped that there will not be too much left open for interpretation! The values presented in this guide represent C-8+ rating or Very Good without the box unless otherwise noted. A C-8+ or Very Good toy will have a slight edge wear, color may not be as bright as an Excellent toy, no parts will be missing, and plastic or paint may be slightly faded. There will be no large dents or damage to the toy.

The prices in this book have been compiled from a combination of factors, including the author's experience, sale prices of specific items from Bradley's Toy Town USA, auction results, typical prices at collectible toy shows, ads appearing in collectible periodicals, dealer price lists, and extensive correspondence with collectors involved in buying, trading, and selling. Keep in mind that prices vary by regions and supply and demand. Ever increasing demands for scarcer items or a newly discovered warehouse find may have an upward or downward effect on prices, therefore it is imperative to keep in mind that this book serves as a guide and does not set the market value. Collectibles, like the stock market, work on the premise that the item is only worth what someone is willing to pay. Boxes can increase the value of a toy by as much as 20 to 40 percent. Although we have listed colors of the pieces, it is very important to note that 50 percent of the time there were no standards to the color of a figure or accessories used in any of the playsets. The colors of figures and accessories were obtained from Fisher-Price catalogs, boxes opened for the first time since they were sealed, salesmen's product sheets, and fellow collectors. A figure could have been blue in one set and red in the next one. A chair or table set could have been red, brown or yellow in any of the playsets. You will note a repetition of some toy numbers. After a toy was out of production, its number could have been assigned to a new toy. At other times the same toy may have been renumbered. We make note of this by indicating (See also #____). The date on the toy is the patent date and is not necessarily the date the toy was issued. It may have been issued that year, the next year, or several years later. The date on the toy cannot be used to judge its rarity as some of the toys were made for 20 years or longer but may be stamped with a 1964 patent date.

In the 1970s Fisher-Price stamped a capital letter followed by a number for better quality control. These represent the month and year of production. For example, "X 9" means the toy was made in December of 1979. Below is a complete list of these letter codes.

January	A	July	K
February	B	August	M
March	C	September	P
April	D	October	S
May	E	November	T
June	H	December	X

Fisher-Price Collectors Club

In 1993 a woman with a true love of Fisher-Price toys wanted to get other people who collected Fisher-Price toys together. She began the Fisher-Price Collectors Club, a non-profit entity that produces a quarterly newsletter appropriately named the "Gabby Goose." Its features include the history of Fisher-Price, articles about our favorite toys, and even a collector's corner. The annual membership dues are $20.00 at the time of this publication. Its annual meeting is held during ToyFest in East Aurora, N.Y. Since the inception of the club, it has grown to over 500 members! For your convenience a club application with additional information has been included in the back of the book. If additional copies are needed please contact Jeanne Kennedy at Fisher-Price Club, 1442 N. Ogden, Mesa, AZ 85205.

Toy Town Museum

Many people have collected toys for years, but in 1987 in the small town of East Aurora, N.Y., home of the renowned Fisher-Price toys, something happened. A small group of East Aurora's merchants, professionals, and citizens met with then Chamber of Commerce head Jim Berg. Their purpose was to discuss the possibility of creating an exciting attraction that would bring visitors to East Aurora as well as provide an interesting place for the townspeople to enjoy. Since East Aurora was the birthplace of Fisher-Price, it was only natural that the attraction be built around toys and children. Thus was born the idea of Toy Town USA, a non-profit organization dedicated to

Open Monday – Saturday 10 – 4
Free Admissions – Donations Accepted

Featuring
Special Exhibits
of Toys from the Past

Toy Town Museum

636 Girard Ave.   P.O. Box 238
East Aurora, NY 14052

Located on the Fisher-Price campus
in historic East Aurora

Phone (716) 687-5151   Fax (716) 5098
www.ToyTownUSA.com

Toy Town is an independent non-profit organization

the creation of a museum and Children's Hands-on Center, where children of all ages could see collections of classic old toys and, in a hands-on way, learn how they work.

The dream had begun!

To generate funds to seed the start and nurture the fulfillment of their dream, the group came up with the idea of a special weekend event to draw local residents as well as those of surrounding communities. They called the event ToyFest and created activities appealing to all members of the family. Some of the events are a parade, carnival rides, kids' space, and a 10K race. They also approached Fisher-Price and contracted them to make a limited production run of one of the old classic toys, which would be sequentially numbered and uniquely collectible.

Over the years these toys have increased in value remarkably; several are worth more than twenty times their original price.

This Toy Town Museum is the result of years of dedication and support by many individuals and businesses. It is by no means the end of their dreams, but, even at this stage, it is beyond their wildest imagination and expectations. It is a world-class facility in a small community filled with historical charm and is attracting national recognition and attention.

ToyFest is a carnival-type celebration created to explore a child's desire for learning through the love of toys and the influence they had in a child's life. ToyFest had its first festival and with that a new era of collectible Fisher-Price Toys began. Buzzy Bee was the first toy reproduced by Fisher-Price in a limited edition. Since 1987 and every year after, there has been a special toy produced just for ToyFest by Fisher-Price in a limited edition of 5,000. These toys are not always exact replicas of toys past; they have minor variations, such as size or plastic wheels instead of wooden.

The museum is a great place for new and old collectors alike to see what kind of legacy Herman Fisher and Irving Price left behind. Not only do they have many of the greatest toys ever made, but they have a rotating toy display, a library where information can be obtained from books, magazines, video tapes, and research done by Jack Murray, Bruce Fox, Bruce Inglis, Larry Davis, Stirling Muck, and Brad Cassity. The museum also has a video room, consignment shop, and a large toy store. The museum would like to thank Fisher-Price museum visitors, toy lovers who loan their collections for display, the volunteers, and all the others who help support the museum.

FISHER-PRICE TOY STORE

The Fisher-Price Toy store is located below the Toy Town Museum. It is a whopping 9,000 square feet of toys! It features Fisher-Price toys, children's products, and apparel. The store also carries a select inventory of Power Wheels and some Mattel products, including Barbie. There is also a Bits and Pieces wall with parts for new and a few older F-P toys that has great prices.

It is located at Fisher-Price Headquarters 636 Girard Avenue, East Aurora, NY 14052.

Toy Store hours:
Monday-Friday, 10:00am-6:00pm
Saturday, 10:00am-5:00pm
Closed Sunday

ADDITIONAL INFORMATION ON FISHER-PRICE

Fisher-Price puts out a yearly shoppers' guide, a Toyfair catalog, and a Bits and Pieces catalog. To order the catalogs, contact Fisher-Price Consumer Affairs, 636 Girard Ave., East Aurora, NY 14052-1885, phone: 1-800-432-5437.

A Historical, Rarity, Value Guide Fisher-Price 1931 – 1963. 2nd ed., 1991, by John J. Murray & Bruce R. Fox. Books Americana.

Schroeder's Collectible Toys Antique to Modern, Price Guide, 4th ed. Chapter by Brad Cassity. Collector Books.

Are you on-line? One of the better web-sites to go to for Fisher-Price products, information, and resources is www.thisoldtoy.com. They have a lot of in-depth information, pictures, descriptions, and more about almost every Fisher-Price toy ever made! There are also links to other sites, trivia, tidbits, little people I.D. guides, and more! Tell them that Brad sent you!

www.thisoldtoy.com

HISTORY

In 1930, a year when the shadows of the Depression were threatening to darken every corner of American business life, two men and a woman introduced a completely new line of toys into the highly competitive toy industry.

The trio combined diverse manufacturing and retailing experience with an unshakable confidence in the public's willingness to welcome products stamped with the sign of quality. The founder, Herman G. Fisher, had been involved in the manufacturing, selling, and advertising of games produced by All-Fair Toys in Churchville, New York. Fisher attempted to purchase All-Fair in 1930 but was unsuccessful. So he ventured out on his own to start what we know today as Fisher-Price. Fisher met Irving R. Price, an early retiree from one of the country's major variety chain stores, F.W. Woolworth, and Hellen E. Schelle and decided to start a company in East Aurora, New York. Without Price, chief financial backer of the company, the company may have never taken off.

Hellen Schelle, although not known by many Fisher-Price collectors, was the third person who made the company the success it is today. Schelle worked for and later owned the Penny Walker Toy Store in Binghamton, New York. She was the backbone of the company, secretary, treasurer, laborer, and designer. Schelle often teamed up with Margaret Evans Price, Irving Price's wife, to design toys. Margaret Evans Price was a well-known artist, illustrator, and author of children's books and novels. Her paintings have been exhibited at the Albright Art Gallery (Buffalo, N.Y) and the Museum of the New York Historical Society, where a permanent collection of her work is housed. Mrs. Price did most of her work in the Fillmore honeymoon cottage once owned by Millard Fillmore, the 13th president of the United States.

In the latter part of 1930 a decision was made to establish manufacturing headquarters in East Aurora, a small, pleasant village 20 miles southeast of Buffalo. The company purchased a frame and concrete-block structure that was once a private residence — still standing today on Church St. — and began to recruit from the immediate area an employee group that knew virtually nothing about the making of toys. They began work with a faith in the ingenuity of the company principals and a realization that the economic climate of the day would require a unity of purpose if the infant operation were to succeed.

The first year, Fisher-Price began the production and marketing of 16 toys, declared "hopefuls" in the view of unsteady financial conditions. The first company catalog titled "Birth Announcement 16 HOPEFULS to the TOY INDUSTRY" contained a toy-making creed that was to shape policy both in bad and good years. They felt good toy making must be based on fundamental principles. The creed was taken from a quote that reads, each toy should have "intrinsic play value, ingenuity, strong construction, good value for the money and action." This creed is still adhered to today. Their toys were to represent value to the buyer and engage and stimulate children in their early years. From the outset, the company founders demonstrated an understanding of the inclinations of preschoolers. "Children," they wrote, "love best the gay, cheerful, friendly toys with amusing action, toys that appeal to their imagination, toys that DO something new and surprising and funny."

The first toys, and those that followed over the course of the years, reflected this understanding. Included in the new line were toys named "Granny Doodle" and "Doctor Doodle," gaily decorated with bright-colored lithographs. As they were pulled, the beaks moved and the toys quacked merrily. This whimsical, light-hearted element in the first toys became a permanent dimension in the Fisher-Price line.

From 1931 – 1948 the toys were made entirely of wood, enlivened with non-toxic lithographs and finishes, and completed with heavy steel parts. Occasionally rubber, oilcloth or string was also used. The wood was Ponderosa pine, a material that resisted splintering and handled rough treatment from preschoolers. The company now makes toys of plastic materials which are equally durable and long-lasting.

The introduction of plastic was first made in 1949, used first for the beaks on the #799 Quacky Family. Plastic was about to change the manufacturing process; it was cheap, durable, and easy to work with.

Although two-thirds of the company's capital was expended in the first four years, the Fisher-

Price line was beginning to generate customer interest and loyalty. The Depression years were difficult ones, but the company survived. Fisher-Price began to view the future with confidence.

The manufacturing effort concentrated in East Aurora for nearly 25 years during which the company prospered and the name of Fisher-Price gained widespread acceptance. In the late 1940s Fisher-Price started to see a need for a larger plant and office facility. In June of 1950 ground was broken for this plant on Girard Ave., which is still the headquarters for Fisher-Price. In the early 1950s, company officials felt the need for a plastics division. The decision was made to purchase the plastic firm of Trimold, Inc., of Kenmore, New York. Manufacturing operations were conducted there until 1962 when the division was moved to its new plant in Holland, New York. This was a facility that produced a variety of injection and blow-molded plastic toy parts until 1991 when Fisher-Price sold it. Several lines were also in evidence, enabling the plant to complete various assembly procedures. The plant itself was located on a 68-acre tract and had been expanded from 55,000 sq. ft. to 94,000.

In 1966, Fisher resigned as president of the company. Henry H. Coords, formerly of Western Electric, an affiliate of American Telephone and Telegraph Company, was recruited as the new chief executive officer. Fisher stayed actively involved in the company until 1969 when Fisher-Price Toys was acquired by the Quaker Oats Company for $50 million, signaling a new era in the company's history.

In 1968 Fisher-Price introduced a new line of toys that generate one of the greatest impacts of the company's history — Play Family sets. We really need to take a step back in time to the true birth of the Little People. We see the first signs of the Little People in 1950 when Fisher-Price added figures to the toy line with #7 Looky Fire Truck. The Fire Truck is a pull toy with three firemen's heads and plastic fire hats nailed to the truck with the bodies printed on the truck. In 1952 Fisher-Price expanded this idea to #415 Super Jet and #730 Racing Rowboat. This seemed to be a hit with children and Fisher-Price continued this through 1958 with heads that spin, pop up and down, or bounce side-to-side. In 1959 the very first removable figures appeared. John Smith from New York City

designed the lithos of toys as a free-lance artist until November 1962 when he started working for Fisher-Price. Although Smith had never seen a Fisher-Price toy, he visualized the concept of figures with the toys. Smith made several different drawings of the #983 Safety School Bus and submitted them to Fisher Price. The bus had removable round litho covered figures with wooden heads. This toy ended up being a very large seller for Fisher-Price, so they started working on other pull toys with removable figures.

The late Ralph Crawford was one of the first, full-time employed designers at Fisher-Price who played a very important role in the Play Family line. Crawford is credited for creating such toys as the #900 Circus Wagon, #932 Amusement Park, #685 Car & Boat, #686 Car & Camper, #915 Play Family Farm, #952 House, #784 Picture Story Camera, and the Music Box radio line. In 1960 Fisher-Price came out with the #243 Nifty Station Wagon with all-wood rounded shape figure, and included a mom, dad, boy and dog. They also introduced the #168 Snorkey Fire Engine with four removable green figures and dog. In 1961 the Safety School Bus was #984 and had gone through some modifications, now with all-wood figures. The Snorky Fire Engine had also gone through some changes and was renumbered #168. During the entire life of the figures and Little People, the only figures to have arms were the firemen so the figures could hold the hose.

The last toy with these figures was the #990 Safety School Bus in 1962. In 1963 the wood figures were much smaller in size, first introduced in this size in the #932 Amusement Park, a 20-piece playset. These toys are the most sought after toys of Fisher-Price collectors and a single MIB may sell for $250.00 to $1,300.00. There were several other toys made with these figure such as the 1963 #719 Fisher-Price Choo-Choo, 1964 #991 Music Box Shoe, 1965 #979 Dump Trucker, and the 1966 #969 Musical Ferris Wheel. It was not until 1965 that the name "Play Family" first appeared on #136 Lacing Shoe. In 1968, three new playsets featured the name "Play Family," the #685 Car & Boat, #686 Car & Camper, and the #915 Play Family Farm 21-piece playset. Although the plastic farm animals are very realistic, they were originally designed as flat wood litho figures like the #900 Circus animals. In 1980 Fisher-Price changed the

name from "Play Family" to "Little People." Through their first 20 years Fisher-Price produced 80 Play-sets with these figures, all highly sought after by Fisher-Price collectors.

In 1970, an additional plant was purchased in Medina, New York. Once owned by the food processing H.J. Heinz Co., the new facility provided additional fabrication, assembling, and molding capability. Several new buildings have been added to the Medina complex since 1970, including an injection molding area that began operations in 1971 and a giant warehouse completed in 1973. In 1995 the company's My Doll House Bed and My Little Garage Bed were complete sell-outs. This fueled a major turn-around in sales of juvenile products, which doubled for the 1996 year. Medina also is one of the manufacturing sites of the outdoor play equipment, a new line embraced by consumers in 1995.

In November 1972, the company broke ground on a 500,000 sq. ft. manufacturing facility in Murray, Kentucky. Operations of injection molding and blow-molded plastic toys and parts began there in the summer of 1973. In 1980 a 40,000 sq. ft. facility was added for plastic molding capabilities, providing assembly, warehousing, distribution, and molding functions for the Murray plant.

In the 1970s Fisher-Price expanded its product line of preschool toys to crib and playpen products introduced in 1973. Their first year, these toys became the nation's best-selling line.

In 1975 playsets and toys for ages 4-9 were introduced. "Adventure People" sets with more realistic figures and play pieces proved very profitable for the toy giant. Other toys introduced during this period were dolls, trucks, Arts & Crafts, Audio Visual, and Construx.

In the 1980s Fisher-Price had expanded its market to an even broader spectrum to include children's non-toy items, such as furniture, clothing, shoes, strollers, books, and car seats.

In January, 1981, Franklyn S. Barry, Jr., formerly executive vice president of Fisher-Price, was appointed president. Berry succeeded Coords who retired December 31, 1980, after 14 years as president. In early 1983, R. Bruce Sampsell was appointed president of Fisher-Price.

Over the past decade, Fisher-Price expanded manufacturing capability on an international level. In 1972 the company opened facilities in Brownsville, Texas, and Metamoros, Mexico. The Mexico facility used to make all sewn products. In 1977, Fisher-Price acquired Montron Corporation in Chula Vista, California, and its sister facility in Tijuana, Mexico.

Manufacturing for Europe and common markets grew when Fisher-Price restructured in 1975 with a facility in Kaulille, Belgium; in 1977, operations began in Peterlee, England.

In May 1991 Quaker Oats sold Fisher-Price which was then privately held until November 1993. Fisher-Price was then purchased by Mattel, the world's largest toy company. With this purchase many new changes were made at Fisher-Price, the largest being a new $17 million, 12,000 sq. ft team center located behind the most recent structure, a glass office building dating from 1977. The team center brings together the people responsible for creating, designing, and selling Fisher-Price toys with the customer service department. Support services such as packing, the mold shop, and play-lab where children test new toys are also located in the center.

In the 65 years of operation, Fisher-Price has grown to the point where today millions of toys are sold each year, shipped to every state and nearly every country of the world. The company employs some 1,000 workers in East Aurora, who participate fully in a generous profit sharing program. Once highly seasonal, the business has benefited from a well-conceived merchandising program that has succeeded in generating toy sales around the calendar. The development of test stores and other marketing innovations have also enabled Fisher-Price to maintain high trade acceptance on the retail level.

The world's largest manufacturer of preschool toys, Fisher-Price has proved conclusively that quality counts, that bright, durable, safe toys will attract children and their mothers. The red and white scallops that identify each Fisher-Price box represent the awning under which the company has made good the vision of its optimistic founders.

Fisher-Price

Our
Vision

Fisher-Price ... First Choice

Fisher-Price

Mission

Fisher-Price will design, engineer, produce and market the world's best children's products characterized by a tradition of uncompromised safety, quality, durability, innovation, and value.

We will continuously strive to improve our products and services to meet or exceed customer and consumer expectations to succeed as a profitable business.

Fisher-Price

Strategic Objectives

▶ To ensure that Fisher-Price continues to be the most trusted name in children's products.

▶ To increase our worldwide recognition as the leader in children's products.

▶ To provide children with innovative toys that will allow them to have fun and enjoy long-term imaginative play.

▶ To achieve excellent performance through people, Fisher-Price will create an environment of teamwork, empowerment, recognition and personal growth.

▶ To provide our retail customers outstanding service and the opportunity for sales at competitive margins throughout the year.

▶ To enrich the lives of others in our communities, particularly children, by contributing generously of our human and financial resources.

Every product that bears the Fisher-Price name comes with a promise from us. A promise that it is well thought out,

THE FISHER-PRICE PROMISE

well made and good value for your money. This is what we stand for. And over the past sixty years, this has made Fisher-Price the most trusted name in children's products. We do it one product, one child, one parent at a time.

Fisher-Price

May 3, 1994

#107 Music Box Clock-Radio 1971, plays "Hickory Dickory Dock" as hands revolve. Hands also turn manually for teaching time. Colorful litho on back and spring attached aerial with wooden bead. Musical movements could be either Japanese or Swiss. **$5.00.**

Second version 1972 – 1984. Wooden bead was changed to plastic. **$2.00.**

Third version 1978 – 1984. This is a prime example of the changes in toys made over the years. The night shift ran out of red ribbon stock used on the inside edge or rim of the plastic cover to hide the four clips that held it on the radio. This change went unnoticed. The ribbon over the clips was dropped from production to cut costs. **$2.00.**

NOTE: There is one other change in this radio that I have no date for. The wind-up knob on the radio in the box has a yellow arrow showing which way to wind it. The radio pictured outside the box does not have the heat stamped arrow but instead two raised arrows molded into the plastic.

#110 Puppy Playhouse. 1978 – 1980. Soft lovable puppy with foam filled fabric house. Included nylon brush for combing and velcro collar and leash. **$10.00.**

#111 Play Family Merry-Go-Round. 1972 – 1977. Merry-Go-Round revolves to "Skaters Waltz" when wound. Four figures: blue girl with blonde hair, red girl with blonde hair, aqua blue boy with red pot hat, black boy with green base and red cowboy hat. They ride in giraffe, pig, turtle or swan seats. On-off switch controls ride. Musical movements could be either Japanese or Swiss. **$40.00.**
Note: The descriptions of the figures are as pictured in 1972 catalogs and boxes. The figures could be in any color combination.

#112 Changeable Picture Disk Camera. 1968 – 1971. Five picture disks with eight pictures on each disk labeled Animals and Their Babies, Visit to City, Goldilocks and Three Bears, Nursery Rhymes One, and Nursery Rhymes Two. Flash cube with lithos rotates; there is also a brightly colorful litho on back of camera. When lens is turned, disk pops up for changing. Dial on lens changes object's color to red, blue, or yellow. Storage compartment on side for picture disks. **$35.00.**
Note: The boy molded on the plastic is Eric Smith, son of John Smith, former art director. John did most of the art work on the Little People playsets lithos. This image was also used in the #634, #784, and #919.

#114 Two Tune Music Box TV. 1966 – 1983. Plays "London Bridge is Falling Down" and "Row Row Row Your Boat" as litho pictures pass screen. There are three versions of the music box, the first having a wood base and litho on the sides, top, and back. Musical movements could be either Japanese or Swiss. **$10.00.**

Second version. Dates are unknown on these changes. The litho on the back was no longer used and the base is now plastic. **$5.00.**

Third version 1981 – 1983. Stopped using the top litho. **$5.00.**

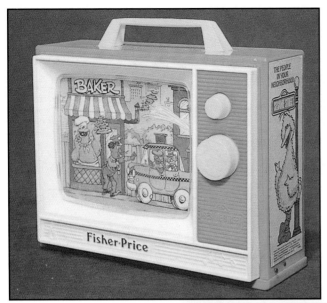

#114 Sesame Street Music Box TV. 1984 – 1987. Plays "The People in Your Neighborhood." All plastic case with litho on sides. Japanese musical movement. **$8.00.**

#117 Play Family Farm Barnyard Friends. 1972 – 1974. 14-piece set sold on a blister card; contains a cow, horse, pig, lamb, brown dog, (with screw-on bellies), six fence sections, watering trough, and two chickens. **$25.00.**

#118 Tumble Tower Game. 1972 – 1975. Tumble ten marbles one-by-one through levels using four different controls. **$10.00.**

#121 Happy Hopper. 1969 – 1971. Push toy. Wood brother, sister, and straight body dog pop up into the air with pop-pop-pop. Plastic housing, wood base. **$20.00.**

1972 – 1976 Dog is no longer a straight bodied figure. **$15.00.**
Note: Even one of these in very poor condition can go for the listed price. Many times one will cut the plastic housing to remove the figure. Condition of figures will drop the listed value.

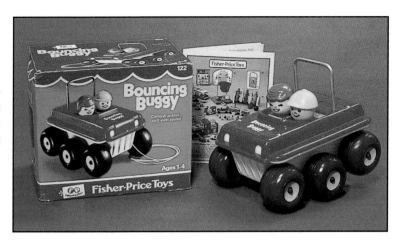

#122 Bouncing Buggy. 1974 – 1979. Six-wheel buggy bounces up and down and makes putt-putt sound when pulled. Can have either a red top and white bottom or vice versa. **$5.00.**

#123 Cackling Hen. 1966 – 1968. Red litho wings flap as feet walk along. Realistic cluck-cluck-cluck. **$40.00.**

#123 Play Family Vehicles Assortment. 1978 only. This set includes all the vehicles in the #124, #125, #126, and #127 sets; all numbered #123.

#124 Play Family Fire Truck. 1979 – 1984. Fire truck with yellow extension ladder and one firefighter with white hands. **$2.00.** MIB. **$10.00.**
Note: The firemen figures are the only ones that had arms. They were designed to hold the fire hose and extension ladders.

Little People Vehicles Fire Truck. 1985 – 1990. Fire truck with yellow extension ladder and one firefighter with white hands. **$2.00.** MIB **$10.00.**

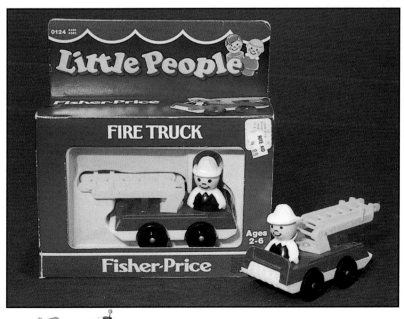

#125 Music Box Iron. 1966 only. Aqua play iron with yellow handle, wheels with rubber treads on bottom activate music box playing "This is how we iron our clothes." Eyes roll up and down and steam button whistles when pushed. Swiss musical movements. **$45.00.**

1967 – 1969 Iron is white with red handle and new litho design was used. Japanese musical movements. **$40.00.**

1969 Iron is yellow with red handle. This is a very rare one to find. **$50.00.**

Note: Fisher-Price used children of employees and non-employees for photographs in catalogs and boxes. The girl here is Lori Inglis, daughter of Bruce Inglis, former U.S. manufacturing vice-president.

#125 Play Family Police Car. 1979 – 1984. Car with police girl figure. **$2.00.** MIB **$10.00.**

Little People Vehicles Police Car. 1985 – 1988. Car with police girl figure and 25 MPH speed sign with a black outline. **$2.00.** MIB **$10.00.**

1989 – 1990 The 25 MPH speed sign no longer had the outline. **$2.00.** MIB **$10.00.**

#126 Play Family Ambulance. 1979 – 1984. Ambulance with white or black driver. **$2.00.** MIB **$10.00.**

#127 Mail Truck. 1979 – 1984. Mail truck has red or blue bugle on the side and gray figure. **$2.00.** MIB **$10.00.**

#130 Wobbles. 1964 – 1967. Dog wobbles when pulled along making an arf-arf-arf sound. Head turns, plastic ears spin, spring tail and vinyl leash **$40.00.**

#131 Milk Wagon. 1964 – 1972. Truck with turquoise bottle carrier and six plastic bottles, four white, one chocolate and one orange, that fit in back of truck. Driver's head looks left and right as bell rings ding-ding-ding. **$50.00.**
Note: Milk carrier that came with this set was never yellow like the #637 version.

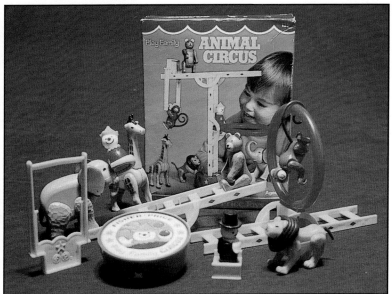

#132 Molly Moo Cow. 1972 – 1978. Squeeze big plastic cow bell. Molly's head moves up and down, making moo-ooo sound, spring-attached tail. **$25.00.**

#135 Play Family Animal Circus. 1974 – 1976. Two ladders with connectors, red hoop, trapeze, and blue platform or tub, H-shaped elephant stand or stool for ringmaster, short-bodied ringmaster, red/yellow clown, bear, monkey, elephant, lion, and giraffe. **$60.00.**

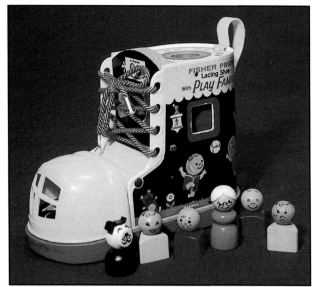

#136 Lacing Shoe with Play Family. 1965 – 1969. 50" long red and white shoe lace, six wood figures: two square red, one boy with smiling face and no hair and girl with smiling face and ribbon in her hair; two triangular yellow, one boy with smiling face and freckles and girl with frowning face and ribbon in her hair; blue mom, white hair with or without glasses/full skirt; and marshmallow-shaped dog. These figures were always all wood. **$60.00.**

Note: For the wood and plastic figures, see #146. This was the first set with "Play Family" name on it.

#138 Pony Chime. 1965 – 1967. Wooden ponies with circus performer litho pulling a musical roller and prancing up and down when pulled. **$40.00.**

#138 Jack-in-the Box Puppet. 1970 – 1973. Push button and puppet pops up with squeeeak sound, lever moves puppet's mouth to make squeak sound. **$30.00.**

#139 Tuggy Tooter. 1967 – 1973. Waterproof for water play or pull play on three wheels. Squeeze life preserver on end of pull tube and smoke stack pops open and whistles toot-toot. Captain sways side to side. **$40.00.**

Note: If the life preserver is split, a little dab of glue over split will reseal it.

#141 Play Family Mini-Bus. 1970 – 1981. Play family vacationers bounce up and down as red bus with white roof rolls along with putt-putt sound. Green dad with painted hair, blue mom with blonde hair, orange boy with painted hair, yellow girl with brown hair, and dog. **$6.00.**
Note: The descriptions of the figures are as pictured in 1970 catalogs and boxes. The figures could be in any color combination.

1982 – 1985 White bus with red roof. **$6.00.**

1986 – 1990 Now called "Mini Van" with newer styled figures. Green dad with black molded hair, red mom with black molded hair, yellow girl with brown molded hair, blue girl with yellow molded hair, and black dog. **$6.00.**
Note: The descriptions of the figures are as pictured in 1986 catalogs and boxes. The figures could be in any color combination.

1988 only. Pampers Promotional. All-yellow van comes with green boy with red cap, yellow girl with brown hair, red mom with blonde hair, blue dad with brown hair, and dog. **$12.00.**
Note: The boy figure is exclusive to this set.

#142 Three Men In A Tub. 1970 – 1973. First version: plastic tub with butcher, baker, and candlestick maker. Blue bell atop the spring mast. **$20.00.**

Second version 1974 – 1975. Same as first with flag in place of bell. **$10.00.**

Third version 1976 – 1985. Bell in center of tub, no longer has spring. **$5.00.**

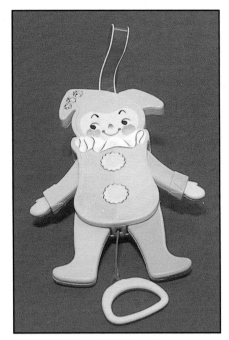

#145 Jolly Jumping Jack. 1970 – 1979. Jumping Jack hangs on crib or playpen. Ring attached to string attracts baby's eye. When pulled, arms and legs move up and down and makes a squeak sound as eyes look left and right. **$5.00.**

#146 Play Family Pull-A-Long Lacing Shoe. 1970 – 1973. 50" long red or blue and white lace, two red square figures, one boy with smiling face and no hair and girl with smiling face and ribbon in her hair; two yellow triangular figures, one boy with smiling face and freckles and girl with frowning face and ribbon in her hair; regular blue mom with white hair with or without glasses; and marshmallow-shaped dog. **$60.00.**

1974 – 1975 Same figures as above but now with plastic heads and wooden bodies. The only exception is the dog; he was always made of wood. **$50.00.**

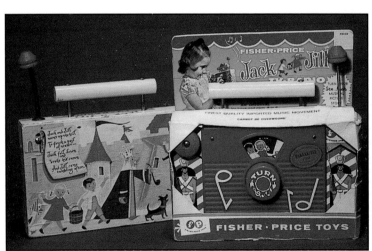

Note: This was the first wind-up musical toy and one of Ralph Crawford's concepts. Back of a non-working radio can be rapped to free up the movement.

#148 "Jack 'n Jill" TV-Radio 1959. Easter 1960. Wooden case and handle with retractable spring antenna with wooden bead, blue plastic face. Musical movements could be either Japanese or Swiss. There was no litho on top or bottom. **$55.00.**

Second version 1960 – 1961. Retractable antenna omitted as well as the knob that moved it up & down. The knob on the left side was now attached with a nail through the front. There was no litho on top or bottom. **$40.00.**

1962 – 1966 The litho was wrapped around all six sides of the radio and the name "Jack N' Jill TV-Radio" that was stamped on the top of the radio was changed to "TV-Radio Fisher-Price Toys." **$40.00.**

1967 only. The plastic frame around the TV window had a raised lip. The wind-up knob now had musical notes instead of the stars from the earlier versions. **$55.00.**

#150 Pop-Up-Pal Chime Phone. 1968 – 1978. When zero is pushed, girl puppet pops up; other buttons make musical chimes sound. The cloth body could be one of many different designs. **$40.00.**
Note: Girl in photo is author's daughter, Christina, age 7.

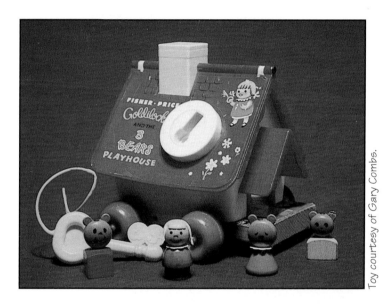

Toy courtesy of Gary Combs.

#151 Goldilocks and Three Bears Playhouse. 1967 – 1971. Roof opens for play fun. When pulled, bell rings and eyes roll; four figures, all-wood blue girl with blonde braids, square, round, and triangular shaped bears with plastic heads fit openings in roof. Plastic key on pull string turns lock on roof making click-click sound. **$60.00.**

#154 "Pop! Goes The Weasel" TV-Radio. 1965 – 1967. Wood case and handle, spring-attached aerial with wooden bead, plastic face, and wood handle. Musical movements could be either Japanese or Swiss. **$25.00.**

1967 only. The plastic frame around the TV window had a raised lip. **$30.00.**

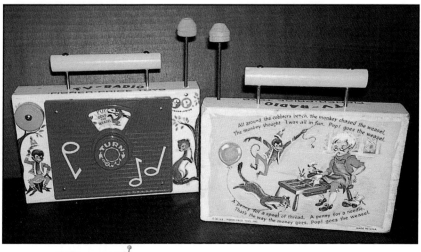

Photo and toy courtesy of Ted Furcht.

#154 Frisky Frog. 1971 – 1983. Squeeze plastic bulb and Frisky makes short or long jumps or sits up. Makes grump sound as he springs into action. **$25.00.**

Photo and toy courtesy of Ted Furcht.

#155 "Jack & Jill" TV-Radio. 1968 – 1970. Has see-through window on back. Litho illustrates nursery rhyme. Wood case with plastic face and handle. Spring-attached aerial with wood bead and click-click turning knob. Musical movements could be either Japanese or Swiss. **$40.00.**

Photo and toy courtesy of Ted Furcht.

#156 "Baa Baa Black Sheep" TV-Radio. 1966 – 1967. Wood case and handle, spring-attached aerial with wooden bead and plastic face. Musical movements could be either Japanese or Swiss. **$50.00.**

#156 Jiffy Dump Truck. 1971 – 1973. Squeeze bulb, dump pops up and down while driver turns head back and forth. **$25.00.**

#158 "Little Boy Blue" TV-Radio. 1967 only. Wood case and handle, spring-attached aerial with wooden bead, plastic face. Musical movements could be either Japanese or Swiss. **$50.00.**

Photo and toy courtesy of Ted Furcht.

Photo and toy courtesy of Ted Furcht.

#158 Katie Kangaroo. 1976 – 1977. Squeeze bulb and Katie hops, swinging her arms, making a boing-boing sound. **$25.00.**

#159 "Ten Little Indians" TV-Radio. 1961 – 1965 & Easter 1966. Wood case and handle, spring-attached aerial with wooden bead and plastic face. Musical movements could be either Japanese or Swiss. **$20.00.**

Photo and toy courtesy of Ted Furcht.

#161 "Old Woman Who Lived in A Shoe" TV-Radio. 1968 – 1970. Has see-through window on back. Litho illustrates nursery rhyme. Wood case with plastic face and handle. Spring-attached aerial with wood bead and click-click turning knob. Musical movements could be either Japanese or Swiss. **$30.00.**

#162 Roly Poly Boats Chime Ball. 1967 – 1969. Sailboat and bell buoys rock back and forth as ball rolls. Makes chime sounds when rolled. **$10.00.**

#164 Mother Goose. 1964 – 1966. Waddles side to side and makes honk-honk sound. Neck swings to and fro. Tail feathers wag. **$35.00.**

#164 Chubby Cub. 1969 – 1972. Bottom is a 6" roly-poly globe with chime sounds. Top is an acrobatic brown bear who lurches and lunges side to side. **$20.00.**

#165 Roly Poly Chime Ball. 1967 – 1985. Swan and hobby-horse rock back and forth as turquoise colored ball rolls. Makes chime sounds when rolled. **$5.00.**

#166 "Farmer-in-The-Dell" TV-Radio. 1963 – 1966. Wood case and handle, spring-attached aerial with wooden bead, plastic face. Musical movements could be either Japanese or Swiss. **$35.00.**

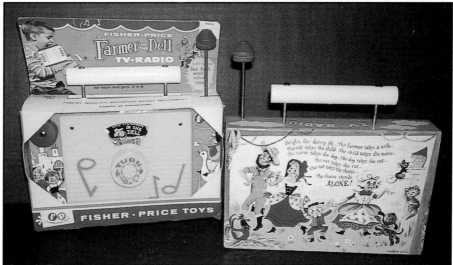

Photo and courtesy of Ted Furcht.

#168 Magnetic Chug-Chug. 1964 – 1969. Engine, gondola, and caboose cars connect with magnetic couplers, makes a chug-chug-chug sound when pulled. **$50.00.**
Note: The gondola has litho on both sides and floor of car.

#166 Piggy Bank. 1981 – 1982. Plastic pink pig with removable hat. **$15.00.**

#170 Change-A-Tune Carousel. 1981 – 1983. Crank handle music box, three plastic children figures: blue girl rust hair, yellow boy, and orange based black boy, with heat stamp hair, three molded records: Do-Re-Mi – Blue Danube, Music Box Dancer – Barbara Allen, Under The Double Eagle – Round The Village. **$30.00**.

Note: The descriptions of the figures are as pictured in 1981 catalogs and boxes. The figures and records could be in any color combination, but not more than one of the same color.

#171 Pull-Along Plane. 1981 – 1988. Sporty plane makes putt-putt sound as propeller spins. **$5.00.**

1989 Number changed (see #2017).

#172 Roly Raccoon. 1980 – 1982. Roly waddles side to side while tail bobs and weaves. **$10.00.**

#175 "Winnie the Pooh" TV-Radio. 1971 – 1973. Sears exclusive. Yellow case with pink handle and knobs. There are lithos on both sides and top of case. The raised lettering and notes are silver. Plays Winnie the Pooh theme song. **$65.00.**

Note: Author's daughter, Dinah, age 9, in photo.

#176 Play Desk. 1972 – 1986. Brownish-red desk with steel magnetic chalkboard. Two slide-in areas on bottom store magnetized alphabet and 14 activity cards. Compartment on top holds numbers 0 – 9, extra letters, chalk, and eraser. Out of nine NRFB sets, all have had the same extra letters of E, I, L, P, N, R, S, and T. **$10.00.**

1987 – 1990 Brown desk and letter tray. **$5.00.**

#177 Oscar the Grouch. 1977 – 1984. Squeeze bulb, lid pops up and Oscar peeks out making "grouch" sound. **$20.00.**

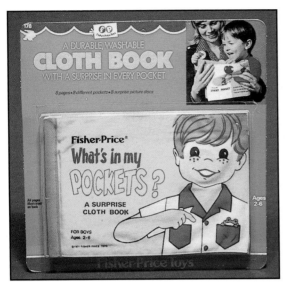

#178 "What's in my Pockets?" A surprise cloth book for boys. 1972 – 1974. Eight-page cloth book with eight different pockets and picture disk for teaching. Each pocket held its own disk depicting a typical object found in a boy's pocket. Disks have no set color and all of them had FP molded on one side and litho on the other. The lithos are of a pocket radio, three marbles, airplane, car, candy bar, watch, acorn, and apple. **$20.00.**
Disks in VG condition. **$3.00 – 5.00 each.**

#179 "What's in my Pockets?" A surprise cloth book for girls. 1972 – 1974. Same as above, but for girls. Disks are hanky, ice cream cone, key, ribbon, comb, money, doll, and ring. **$20.00.**
Disks in VG condition. **$3.00 – 5.00 each.**

#182 Jetliner. 1981 – 1985. Plastic jet with engine-like sound, white and green body with yellow wings, hinged door, and dark blue windshield. Four plastic figures: yellow mom with brown hair, green dad with painted hair, orange boy with painted hair, lime green girl with brown hair, and two pieces of luggage, one square and other round. **$10.00.**

1986 Number changed (see #2360)
Note: The descriptions of the figures are as pictured in 1981 catalogs and boxes. The figures could be in any color combination.

#183 Play Family Fun Jet. 1970 only. First version made for only one year. Did not have a hole for the gas tank on the wing or the tow hole by the front wheel. Plastic red wings with blue jet engines, makes whirring engine sound. Pilot looks left and right. Four wood figures: green dad with heat stamped hair, blue mom with blonde hair, orange boy with heat stamped hair, and blue girl with blonde hair; two pieces of luggage, one round, the other square. **$25.00.**

1971 – 1980 Same as above, but with hole on wing for gas hose and tow hook located behind front wheel. **$15.00.**
Note: The descriptions of the figures are as pictured in 1970 catalogs and boxes. The figures could be in any color combination.

#189 Pull-A-Tune Bluebird Music Box. 1969 – 1979. Hangs on crib or playpen with adjustable plastic strap. Plays "Children's Prayer" when bead is pulled. **$8.00.**

#190 Pull-A-Tune Pony Music Box. 1969 – 1972. Hangs on crib or playpen with adjustable plastic strap. Plays Schubert's "Cradle Song" when bead is pulled. **$15.00.**

#192 School Bus. 1965 – 1969. New version of #990. Wood base bus and driver. Driver looks left and right as bus looks up and down with headlight eyes. Hinged door with swinging stop sign. There are a total of seven figures, three female figures in any color combination body and hair. The two girl figures may or may not have freckles. The mom figure was a blue short body figure with blonde hair. The three male figures were in any color combination body and hair and two may or may not have freckles. One of the boy figures always had the mad face and the other two would have either a cowboy hat, baseball cap, or pan hat in either yellow or red. The dog was brown or light tan. Although this is very unusual, the dog also could have been a black all-wood straight bodied figure with red or blue collar with or without ribs. **$125.00.**

1970 – 1976 The dog was either all-wood or all-plastic black regular shaped figure. **$75.00.**

1977 – 1990 Same bus without swinging stop sign. In later years the driver's head and base of bus were made of plastic. **$10.00.**

Names of figures in the #192 Bus. When figures came on cardboard package: tan or black dog, Fido; mad face boy, Butch; red body girl, Patty; green boy with pot hat, Freckles; short body blue mom, Suzie; green body girl with red hair, Penny.

On the #192 bus box when figures came in plastic bag: green body girl with red hair, Penny; short body blue mom, Suzie; red boy with yellow cowboy hat, Bill; green boy with red pot hat, Freckles; mad face boy with red baseball cap, Butch; red girl with blond hair, Patty; and black dog, Fido.

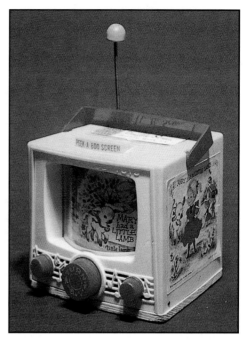

#194 Push Pullet. 1971 – 1972. Chicken makes real-istic cluck-cluck-squawk sound as wings whirl. All plastic with 16" push stick. **$25.00.**

#195 "Mary Had A Little Lamb" Double Screen TV Music Box. 1965 – 1968. Music box TV set. As music plays, nursery rhyme words and pictures revolve across screen. "Peek-A-Boo" screen on top of case. Make-believe channel selector and on-off knobs click-click. Has litho on the top and both sides and the musical movements could be either Japanese or Swiss. **$30.00.**

#196 "Hey Diddle Diddle" Double Screen TV Music Box. 1964 only. As music plays, nursery rhyme words and pictures revolve across screen. "Peek-A-Boo" screen on top of case. Make-believe channel selector and on-off knobs click-click. Has litho on top and both sides. Side lithos depict Mother Goose, Mary and Lamb, school house, boy, girl, and castle. The musical movements could be either Japanese or Swiss. **$50.00.**

1965 – 1970 New litho design now depicts Cat and Fiddle, Dog, Cow jumping over Moon, Spoon and Plate. **$30.00.**

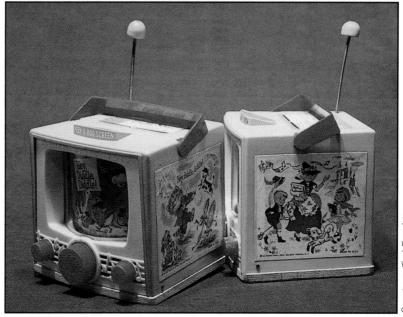

Courtesy Ted Furcht.

#200 Mary Doll. 1974 – 1977. Vinyl face and hands with cloth body, 13" tall, rooted hair. Outfit with velcro tape. Doll has permanent color coordinated outfit of pajamas or tights. She is wearing a removable apron and skirt. **$25.00.**

#201 Jenny. 1974 – 1976. Same description as #200. Wistful expression. She is wearing a flowered print dress with skirt. **$25.00.**

#202 Natalie. 1974 – 1976. Same description as #200. Dimpled face. She is wearing a removable skirt and bonnet. **$25.00.**

#203 Audrey. 1974 – 1976. Same description as #200. Mischievous eyes. She is wearing removable bib blue jeans. **$25.00.**

#204 Baby Ann. 1974 – 1976. Same description as #200 with flesh-colored fabric covering. She is wearing a removable nightgown and diaper. **$25.00.**

#204 Musical Baby Ann. Made some time between 1975 and 1976. This doll was never given a number and only 300 were made because of costs. It is the same as the #204 doll with a music box in her back. **$250.00.**

#205 Elizabeth. 1974 – 1976. Black doll. Same description as #200. Elizabeth is a heartbreaker. She is wearing a removable skirt. **$25.00.**

#206 Joey. 1975 – 1976. Boy doll, 13" tall, vinyl face and hands, cloth body, rooted hair. He is wearing removable football jacket and sneakers with lace and tie feature. **$25.00.**

#205 My Friend Mikey. 1982 – 1984. The only male My Friend doll. Came with blue jeans, polo shirt, baseball jacket, and sneakers. **$30.00.**

#206 My Friend Nicky. 1985 only. There are not too many of these dolls. They were not a big hit and were not in the 1985 catalogs. The only advertisement features two dolls and offers the different outfits, not the doll. Dressed in a blue and white striped knit sweater with monogrammed Mandy megaphone. Matching skirt, white socks, sneakers, head band, and two pom-pons. **$30.00.**

#207 My Sleepy Baby. 1979 – 1980. Doll with closing eyes. Permanently attached pink stretch suit and bonnet. Bunny playmate attached to her arm with elastic and simple outfit pattern. **$20.00.**

#209 My Friend Jenny. 1984 – 1985. Jenny is ready for aerobics in her magenta and turquoise sweatshirt, mini skirt, braided headband, tights, leg warmers, striped sneakers, and gold purse. **$20.00.**

#208 Honey. 1977 – 1980. Boy doll, same description as #200. Yellow and white print pajamas. **$20.00.**

#210 My Friend Mandy. 1977 – 1978. Soft cloth body with vinyl arms and legs. Came dressed in a straw hat, pink party dress, stretchy tights, and white slip-on shoes. Also came with nightgown and booklet, "Caring For My Friend Mandy," full of details on washing, shampooing, and grooming. Also includes a simple pattern. **$20.00.**

#211 My Friend Mandy. 1979 – 1981. The doll is the same as #210 but the dress has a flowered pattern. This was a number change only. **$20.00.**

#212 My Friend Jenny. 1979 – 1981. Same as #210 with puffy-sleeved white blouse, jumper, wide brimmed straw hat, tights, and brown shoes. **$20.00.**

#215 My Friend Mandy. 1982 – 1983. Up-to-date look. Navy blue and white polka-dotted dress, red straw hat with white ribbon, and red shoes. **$20.00.**

Note: Outfits made from 1977 – 1978 came in a ¾" thick box. Outfits made from 1979 – 1984 came on a blister pack.

#215 Patio Party Denim Outfit. 1977 – 1978. Denim skirt with pretty contrasting ruffles and print blouse. **$10.00.**

#216 Sleigh Ride Ensemble Outfit and Pattern. 1977 – 1978. Hat and coat with plush trim uses hook and eye fasteners. **$10.00.**

#217 Country Fair Bib-Jeans Outfit and Pattern. 1977 – 1978. Denim bib-jeans with snap button decoration and handy pocket. Short sleeved knit shirt with velcro fasteners. **$10.00.**

#218 Town & Country Pantsuit Outfit and Pattern. 1977 – 1978. Pants with elastic waistband, three fasteners on matching shirt jacket, ascot for scarf or belt, and fashionable clogs. **$10.00.**

#216 My Friend Mandy. 1984 only. Mandy as all-American cheerleader. Dressed in a blue and white striped knit sweater with monogrammed Mandy megaphone. Matching skirt, white socks, sneakers, head band, and two pom-pons. **$30.00.**

#217 My Friend Jenny. 1982 – 1983. Brunette hair doll with yellow dress, white straw hat with yellow ribbon, and white shoes. **$20.00.**

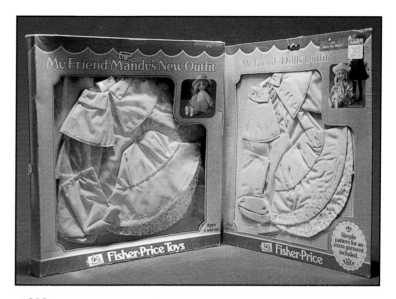

#219 Rainy Day Slicker Outfit. 1978 – 1980. Slicker with matching hat and boots. **$10.00.**
Note: Outfits made from 1977 – 1978 came in a ¾" thick box. Outfits made from 1979 – 1984 came on a blister card.

#218 My Friend Becky. 1982 – 1984. Red hair, green eyes, and freckled face. Green dress, white straw hat with green ribbon, and white shoes. **$20.00.**

#220 Springtime Tennis Outfit and Pattern. 1978 – 1982. Shirt, shorts, sneakers, and tinted visor. **$10.00.**
Note: Outfits made from 1977 – 1978 came in a ¾" thick box. Outfits made from 1979 – 1984 came on a blister pack.

#221 Party Time Dress Outfit and Pattern. 1978 – 1979. Full-length gown with shirred bodice, puffed sleeves, and party shoes. **$10.00.**
Note: Outfits made from 1977 – 1978 came in a ¾" thick box. Outfits made from 1979 – 1984 came on a blister pack.

#222 Let's Go Camping Outfit and Pattern. 1978 – 1979. Plaid flannel shirt. Cotton twill pants, shoes, and back card. **$10.00.**
Note: Outfits made from 1977 – 1978 came in a ¾" thick box. Outfits made from 1979 – 1984 came on a blister pack.

#223 Jumper and Blouse Outfit and Pattern offer. 1979 – 1982. Blue jumper with blouse and tie. **$10.00.**

#224 Jogging Outfit and Pattern offer. 1979 – 1982. Warm-up pants and jacket. **$10.00.**

#225 Sweater-Coat Outfit and Pattern offer. 1979 – 1984. Sweater coat matching hat, belt, and slacks. **$10.00.**

#226 Footwear and Pattern. 1979 – 1980. Sneakers, fashion boots, and two pairs of tights, white and navy blue. **$12.00.**

#228 Ballerina Outfit & Pattern offer. 1980 – 1985. Pink body with matching tights, slippers, and silver tiara. **$10.00.**

#229 Knickers Outfit and Pattern offer. 1980 – 1982. Knickers, beret, blouse, and socks. **$10.00.**

#230 Winter Wear Outfit and Pattern offer. 1981 – 1984. Ski vest, slacks, and fur boots. **$10.00.**

#231 Roller Skating Outfit and Pattern offer. 1981 – 1985. Yellow skating outfit with shoes, and roller skates with working wheels. **$10.00.**

#232 Bedtime Outfit and Pattern offer. 1982 – 1983. Pink flowered nightgown, rose-colored robe, and plush slippers. **$10.00.**

#233 Baseball Outfit and Pattern offer. 1982 – 1984. Red and white shirt, pants, socks, baseball glove, and cap. **$10.00.**

#235 Four Seasons Fashions Outfits. 1979 – 1982. 16-page book with four patterns, tips on making accessories, and the tale of two good friends. **$10.00.**

#237 Sunshine Party Dress Outfit and Pattern. 1984 only. Yellow gingham pinafore dress, matching straw hat, and white shoes. **$10.00.**

#238 Valentine Party Dress Outfit and Pattern. 1984 – 1985. Blue polka-dot bib dress, straw hat, and red shoes. **$10.00.**

#242 Billie. 1979 – 1980. 8" doll with removable hat and skirt. **$10.00.**

#240 Mikey. 1979 – 1980. 8" doll with removable baseball hat and jacket. **$10.00.**

#241 Muffy. 1979 – 1980. 8" doll with removable hat and skirt. **$10.00.**

#243 Bobbie. 1979 – 1980. 8" doll with removable hat and skirt. **$10.00.**

Box for #240 – #243 shown with #242 Billie.

#244 Bundle-Up Baby. 1980 – 1982. Baby with attached jump suit and hood. Padded bassinet and quilted coverlet. **$20.00.**

#250 Doll House. 1978 – 1980. Three-story with five rooms, spiral staircase, gray siding, litho dad, mom with movable parts, wallpaper, and instruction booklet with hints on decorating. Accessories sold separately. **$40.00.**

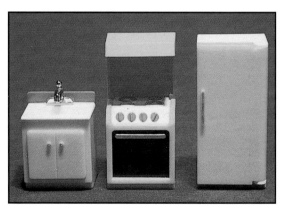

#252 Kitchen Appliances. 1978 – 1984. Oven range with exhaust, refrigerator, and sink. **$8.00.**

#251 Dinette. 1978 – 1983. Pedestal table with four chairs. **$4.00.**

#254 Chair & Fireplace. 1978 – 1982. Chair with cushion and fireplace. **$6.00.**

#253 Bathroom. 1978 – 1984. Green sink, toilet, and shower stall. **$6.00.** (See #4328)

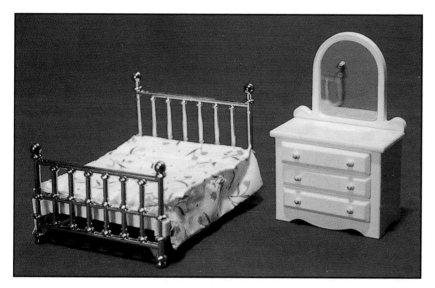

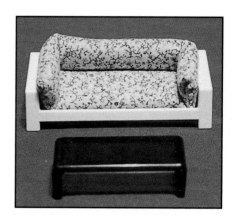

#256 Living Room Set. 1978 – 1982. Sofa with brown cushion, and coffee table. **$6.00.** (See #269)

#255 Bedroom Set. 1978 – 1984. Brass bed with cover, white dresser with mirror and three drawers. **$6.00.**

1985 only. Same set with bed cover matching the white and light blue dresser with pink print. **$8.00.**

#257 Baby's Room. 1978 – 1984. Baby, white crib, dresser with blue doors, and rocking horse. **$10.00.**

1985 only. Same set. Baby, dresser with light blue doors, and white crib with pink print. **$15.00.** (See #4325)

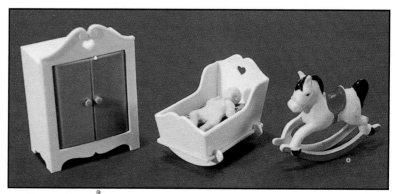

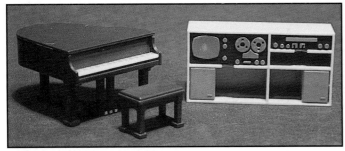

#258 Music Room. 1978 – 1981. Dark brown grand piano with stool, and stereo center. **$8.00.**

#259 Bed Set. 1979 – 1980. Bunk beds with mattress and female figure. **$6.00.**

#260 Patio Set. 1979 – 1982. Redwood type chair, chaise lounge, grill, and collie dog. **$8.00.**

1985 Same set made of light brown. **$8.00.** (See #272 & #4325)

#262 Clock & Rocker. 1980 – 1982. Brown Grandfather clock with movable hands and brown rocking chair. **$5.00.** (See #271 & 273)

#261 Desk Set. 1980 – 1983. Tan roll-top desk with swivel chair and spinning globe. **$6.00.**

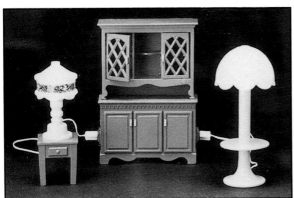

#263 Deluxe Decorator Set With Lights. 1981 – 1984. Brown hutch with compartment for AA batteries, two lamps, tulip white shaded floor lamp and Tiffany-like lamp on brown table. **$10.00.**

#264 Dining Room Set. 1981 – 1984. Butterfly drop-leaf table with white bowl and four straight backed chairs. **$5.00.**

1985 only. Same set with pink chair cushions and pink bowl on table. **$8.00.** (See #4325)

#265 Doll House Family. 1981 – 1985. Dad, mom, son, and daughter. **$2.50 each.**

#268 Wing Chair and Rug Set. 1982 – 1983. Blue wing-backed chair with footstool, large potted plant, and blue, green, orange, and white Oriental rug. **$8.00.**

1985 only. Same set with light blue chair and footstool, light blue and pink print Oriental rug, and plant. **$12.00.** (See #4325)

#269 Sofa Base and Cushion. 1983 – 1985. No longer sold in a set. **$4.00.**

#270 Fireplace. 1983 – 1985. No longer sold in a set. **$3.00.**

#271 Clock. 1983 – 1985. No longer sold in a set. **$3.00.**

#272 Lounge and Grill. 1983 – 1984. No longer sold in a set. **$4.00.**

#273 Rocker. 1983 – 1984. No longer sold in a set. **$4.00.**

#274 Dog. 1983 – 1985. No longer sold in a set. **$2.50.**

#275 Man. 1983 – 1985. No longer sold in a set. **$2.50.**

#276 Woman. 1983 – 1985. No longer sold in a set. **$2.50.**

#277 Boy. 1983 – 1985. No longer sold in a set. **$2.50.**

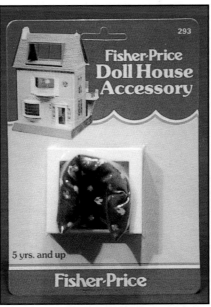

#278 Girl. 1983 – 1985. No longer sold in a set. **$2.50.**

#279 Chair Base and Cushion. 1983 – 1985. No longer sold in a set. **$5.00.**

#287 Tiffany-styled Table Lamp. 1983 – 1984. Brown table and tan lamp. No longer sold in a set. **$5.00.**

1985 only. Pink table and brown lamp. **$8.00.**

#280 Doll House with Lights. 1981 – 1984. This is the same as #250 but is lighted, with litho yellow siding. Has a battery compartment and seven outlets throughout the house for lights and a ceiling light. Comes with ceiling light, table lamp, spiral staircase, construction straps, wallpaper, and decorating/assembly guide. **$50.00.**

#300 Scoop Loader. 1975 – 1977. Construction vehicle with removable round construction figure that fits in driver's seat. Handle for operating scoop, another for dumping load, makes engine sounds. **$25.00.**

#300 Husky Scoop Loader. 1978 only. Construction vehicle with Husky helper that fits in rectangular driver's seat. Handle for operating scoop, another for dumping load, makes engine sounds. **$20.00.**

Toy courtesy of Gary Combs.

#301 Shovel Digger. 1975 – 1977. Construction shovel vehicle with removable round construction figure that fits in driver's seat One handle raises arms, another operates shovel. **$25.00.**

#301 Husky Shovel Digger. 1978 only. Crane shovel vehicle rotates on turret with Husky helper that fits in rectangular driver's seat. One handle raises arms, another operates shovel. **$20.00.**

#302 Dump Truck. 1975 – 1977. Construction truck with removable round figure that fits in driver's seat Dumping action and detachable front shovel for digging or raking. Makes engine sound. **$30.00.**

#302 Husky Dump Truck. 1978 – 1984. Dump truck with dumping action and detachable front shovel for digging or raking. Makes engine sound. Husky figure that fits in rectangular seat. **$20.00.**

#303 The Adventure People Emergency Rescue Truck. 1975 – 1978. Rescue truck with extendible boom and siren button, green stretcher, oxygen tank, blue figured man, Tom, and woman, Nancy. **$15.00.**

#304 The Adventure People Wild Safari Set. 1975 – 1978. Orange two-seater Jeep with passenger bench and trailer, cloth stockade fence, four figures, Safari Jim, Mom, Johnny, and Jenny, movie camera, five animals, gorilla, zebra, lion, tiger, giraffe, collapsible cloth tent, two cages, capture net, and ladder. **$55.00.**

#305 The Adventure People Air-Sea Rescue Copter. 1975 – 1980. Helicopter and gold color raft, two gold color figures, Jess and Roger. **$15.00.**

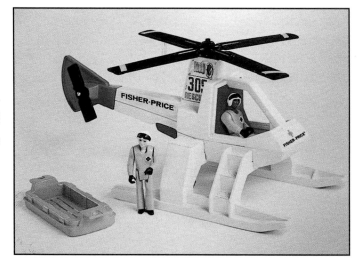

#306 The Adventure People DareDevil Sport Plane. 1975 – 1980. Orange and white plane with gold pilot. **$8.00.**

#307 Adventure People Wilderness Patrol. 1975 – 1979. Bush plane, pontoon boat with motor, and all-terrain vehicle carry three crew members, ranger, Scott; pilot, Greg; woodsman, Red; and collie dog. Two sleeping bags and climbing rope with hooks. **$30.00.**

#308 Adventure People The Super Speed Racer. 1976 – 1979. Red or white Speed Racer with driver Buzz. **$8.00.**

#309 Adventure People TV Action Team. 1977 – 1978. Blue van, main camera that focuses, seven-piece tower for camera, mini-cam, mike-pack, three cables. Announcer, Carole; technician, Kirk; and director, Jeff. **$60.00.**

#310 Adventure People Sea Explorer. 1975 – 1980. Motor boat, sea sled, two divers, Dave and Mary, skis, tow rope, two clip-on scuba tanks, and Splash the dolphin. **$25.00.**

#311 Bulldozer. 1976 – 1977. Construction bulldozer with a spring-loaded shovel and removable round construction figure that fits in driver's seat. Storag box, tow bar extends to 5½", makes engine noise. **$25.00.**

#311 Husky Bulldozer. 1978 – 1979. Bulldozer with spring-loaded shovel on the front and rectangular driver's seat. Storage box, tow bar extends to 5½", makes engine sound. Husky helper that fits in rectangular driver's seat. **$20.00.**

#312 Adventure People Northwoods Trailblazer. 1977 – 1982. Orange and yellow Jeep, two-piece cloth tent, canoe with two oars, clip-on motor. Explorer, Brad, and Hawk, the excellent guide. **25.00.**

#313 Roller Grader. 1977 only. An earth-packing truck with grader for leveling bumps. Removable round construction figure fits in driver's seat. **$25.00.**

#313 Husky Roller Grader. 1978 – 1980. An earth-packing grader with tilting up grader for leveling bumps. Makes engine sound and includes Husky helper that fits into rectangular seat. **$20.00.**

#314 Husky Boom Crane. 1978 – 1982. Rugged construction truck. Crank reels the cable with either a weighted hook, removable magnet, or open-sided bucket with claw-tooth bottom. Push-button handle raises and lowers or locks boom. Third handle swivels the turret. Makes engine sounds and has a Husky helper that fits in rectangular driver's seat. **$25.00.**

#315 Husky Cement Mixer. 1978 – 1982. Turn-crank drum revolves to mix up dirt. Pull big handle and dump dirt down free-standing chute. Removable water tank stores water. Makes engine sound and has Husky helper that fits in rectangular driver's seat. **$30.00.**

#316 Husky Tow Truck. 1978 – 1980. Winch chain is adjustable by sliding lock up and down. Converts into a pickup truck when winch is pulled out. Has Husky helper and makes engine sound. **$15.00.**

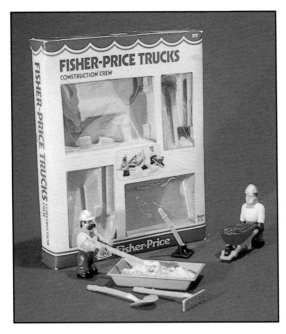

#317 Husky Construction Crew. 1978 – 1980. Husky helpers with hoe, shovel, rake, wheelbarrow, movable tamper, and water trough. **$30.00.**

#318 The Adventure People Daredevil Sports Van. 1978 – 1982. Customized van, parachute with harness that fits into a bag, racing kayak with paddle, racing bike with rack that attaches to back of van, and two helmeted figures. **$30.00.**

#319 Husky Hook and Ladder. 1979 – 1985. Two-piece fire truck with pivoting extension ladder, spotlight, and removable water nozzle. Chief and firefighter. **$25.00.**

#320 Husky Race Car Rig. 1979 – 1982. Race car, flatbed truck, pit stop rack, and Husky driver with stripes and helmet. **$30.00.**

1985 Number changed (see #4508)

#322 The Adventure People Dune Buster. 1979 – 1982. Green off-road vehicle, flag, spare gas tank, driver wearing boots, glasses, and hat. **$15.00.**

Note: In 1979 – 1980 Fisher-Price redesigned most of the pre-1980 Adventure Series boxes and blister packs. This box went from the plain three-color look to a full-color jungle design.

#321 Husky Firefighters. 1979 – 1980. Firemen with fire ax, shovel, crowbar, stretcher, backpack fire extinguisher, and clip-on oxygen tank. **$30.00.**

#323 The Adventure People Aero-Marine Search Team. 1978 – 1983. Nine-piece set includes helicopter with hook and pilot, submarine with diver in wet suit, octopus, treasure chest, cage with cradle, and scuba tank. **$25.00.**

#325 The Adventure People Alpha Probe. 1980 – 1984. Space ship with three buttons, one for rocket sound, communication sounds, and emergency light with sound. Smaller ship, "Alpha Recon," inside cargo bay, life support cable, male and female figures in space suits. **$25.00.**

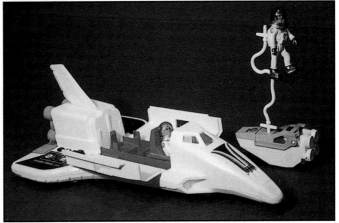

#326 The Adventure People "Alpha Star." 1983 – 1984. Battery-operated Rover and trailer with forward, reverse, and steering action. Radar/camera and antenna rotate. Launching chamber with robot. Also includes alien creature and decal sheet. **$30.00.**

#327 Husky Load Master Dump. 1984 only. Ten-wheel semi rig with detachable white cab for access to driver's seat and red working dump trailer. Figure with red baseball hat. **$30.00.**

#328 Husky Highway Dump Truck. 1980 – 1984. Handle lifts the dump box and locks it in the dumping position. Tailgate opens to release the load. Included is a shovel and rake that fit into top of truck and Husky helper that fits in rectangular driver's seat. **$25.00.**

#329 Husky Dozer Loader. 1980 – 1984. Three-way handle action, back handle to push dirt piles, second handle to raise and lock bucket in up position, and third handle to dump the load. Includes a Husky helper that fits in rectangular driver's seat. **$15.00.**

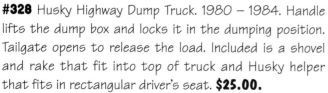

#330 Husky Rodeo Rig. 1980 – 1984. Gold and green stake truck, Husky wearing a 10-gallon hat, with white horse and saddle. **$20.00.**

1985 Number change (see #4516)

#331 Husky Farm Set. 1981 – 1983. Longhorn bull, red tractor, wagon with four removable gray sides, and Husky farmer in bib overalls and straw hat. **$25.00.**

#332 Husky Police Patrol Squad. 1981 – 1984. Police car and motorcycle with engine sounds, helicopter with spinning rotors. Policeman and motorcycle cop. **$25.00.**

1985 Number changed (see #4512)

#333 The Adventure People Wheelie Dragster. 1981 – 1984. Black or white dragster with friction motor and race car driver figure. **$15.00.**

#334 The Adventure People Sea Shark. 1981 – 1984. Blue and white patrol boat, vinyl shark, two divers in wet suits, two scuba tanks, and two buoys. **$25.00.**

#335 The Adventure People Moto Cross Team. 1983 – 1984. Van with ramp tailgate and roof rack. Dirt bike and two gas cans fit on roof rack. Race driver and teammate figures. **$20.00.**

#336 Husky Fire Pumper. 1983 – 1984. Red fire truck uses real water with hand-operated pump. Has two extension ladders and firemen. **$20.00.**

1985 Number changed (see #4508)

#337 Husky Rescue Rig. 1982 – 1983. Rescue truck with opening rear ramp, fire extinguisher, oxygen mask, and stretcher with folding legs and rolling wheels. Two figures, driver and victim. **$25.00.**

#338 Husky Power Tow Truck. 1982 – 1984. Wind-up motor that runs for 40 feet and makes motor sounds as it goes. Husky figure included. **$25.00.**

#339 Husky Power and Light Service Rig. 1983 – 1984. Nine-piece playset. Emergency truck with lights on roof, bucket, and boom, trailer, spotlight, two pylons, air hose with jackhammer, safety barricade, and road sign. Bearded Husky figure. **$30.00.**

#340 Fisher-Price Little Truck. 1980 – 1984. Orange and yellow bulldozer with spring-loaded action and any color worker with chrome-like hard hat. **$3.00.**

#341 Fisher-Price Little Truck. 1980 – 1984. Orange and yellow front-end loader with spring-loaded action and any color worker with chrome-like hard hat. **$3.00.**

#342 Fisher-Price Little Truck. 1980 – 1984. Orange and yellow dump truck with spring-loaded action and any color worker with chrome-like hard hat. **$3.00.**

#343 Fisher-Price Little Truck. 1980 – 1984. Orange and yellow forklift with spring-loaded action, pallet, crate, and any color worker with chrome-like hard hat. **$6.00.**

#344 Copter Rig. 1981 – 1984. Green and white truck with lowboy trailer and slim yellow copter. Two figures: one tan with silver hard hat and one blue with blue cap. Set with pictured figures only. **$15.00.**
(Not the same as #2449)

#345 Boat Rig. 1981 – 1984. Blue and white truck with lowboy trailer and plastic boat. Two figures, one green with a silver hard hat, and one white with blue hat. Set came with pictured figures only. **$15.00.**

#346 Little People Vehicles Fire Truck. 1983 – 1989. Red hook 'n ladder fire truck with yellow stabilizers, white extension ladder, and two firefighters with silver hats and white hands. **$15.00.**

#347 Little People Vehicles Indy Racer. 1983 – 1990. Yellow and white truck and trailer with tilting action, race car, black driver with helmet, and blue figure with white or blue hat. **$8.00.**

#350 The Adventure People Rescue Team. 1976 – 1979. Rolling stretcher, rescue blanket, clip-on first aid pack, Mike, and Susan. **$18.00.**

#351 The Adventure People Mountain Climbers. 1976 – 1979. Climbers Mike and Jan, backpack with two sleeping bags, climbing harness, and 28" rope with hook. **$20.00.**

#351 Speed Commanders Chevy Stepside Pickup. 1985 only. Steerable battery-operated vehicle with automatic shut-off feature. **$20.00.**

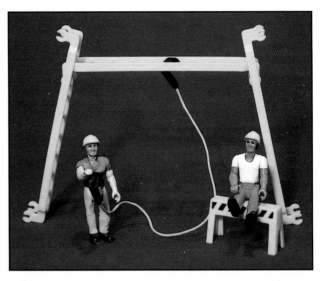

#352 The Adventure People Construction Workers. 1976 – 1979. Barney and Frank with hard hats, three-piece ladder, 15" cable with hooks, and barricade sign. **$20.00.**

#352 Speed Commanders Jeep CJ-7 Renegade. 1985 only. Steerable battery-operated vehicle with automatic shut-off feature, steerable. **$15.00.**

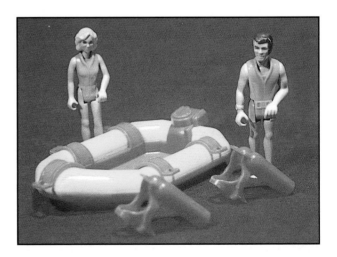

#353 The Adventure People Scuba Divers. 1976 – 1981. Divers Matt and Becky with scuba tanks and diving raft. **$15.00.**

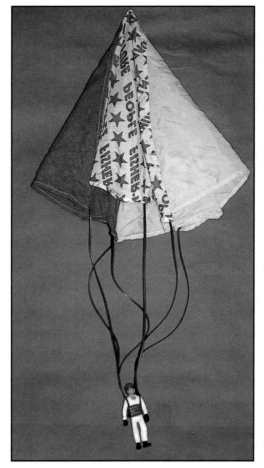

#354 The Adventure People DareDevil Skydiver. 1977 – 1981. Skydiver in jumpsuit with chute and detachable harness. **$10.00.**

#355 The Adventure People White Water Kayak. 1977 – 1980. Kayak, boater in life vest, paddle, and three buoys. **$15.00.**

#356 The Adventure People Cycle Racing Team. 1977 – 1984. Cycle with side car and two racing drivers. **$10.00.**

#357 The Adventure People FireStar 1. 1980 – 1984. Either black or white and silver rocket sled, life support cable, and pilot in black space suit. **$15.00.**

#358 The Adventure People Deep Sea Diver. 1980 – 1984. Diver in brass helmet, dive float with flag and 10" air hose, and octopus. **$15.00.**

#359 The Adventure People Land Speed Racer. 1981 – 1984. Yellow salt flat car and driver. **$8.00.**

#360 The Adventure People Alpha Recon. 1982 – 1984. Red four-wheel vehicle with rotating radar and figure in white space suit with vision glasses. **$15.00.**

#367 The Adventure People Kit Turbo Hawk. 1982 – 1983. Adventure kit assembles with screw. Includes plastic parts, screw key, stick-on labels, instructions, and figure. Blue and white jet plane with opening canopy and display stand, white jet pilot. **$15.00.**

#368 The Adventure People Kit Alpha Interceptor. 1982 – 1983. White two-stage space vehicle, red astronaut, and tether. **$15.00.**

#369 The Adventure People Kit Ground Shaker. 1982 – 1983. Funny car with working friction motor and race driver figure. Body shell raises to show off chrome engine. **$15.00.**

#370 The Adventure People Kit Trail Boss. 1983. Only 4 x 4 pickup truck with sun-roof, roll bar, folding tail gate, decal sheet, and Western figure. **$20.00.**

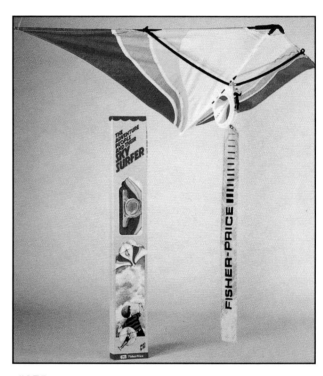

#375 The Adventure People Sky Surfer. 1978 only. A plastic and nylon hang glider or kite. Snaps together and comes with 70" of string and floor display stand. **$25.00.**
Note: This toy was pulled from the market in April of 1978 due to some defects.

#377 The Adventure People Astro Knight. 1979 – 1980. Foam plastic space glider with 10" wing span and Astro Knight figure. Came in two different colors. Figure colors must match glider colors. **$15.00.**

#392 Action Figure Assortment. 1978 – 1979. Each case contained one of 12 different figures on a three-color blister pack. This picture is of a store display and only shows 18 of 36 different figures sold during this period. They are **#354** DareDevil Skydiver, **#305** Air-Sea Rescue Copter Jess & Roger, **#304** Wild Safari, Safari Jim, Mom, Johnny & Jenny, **#309** TV Action Team, announcer Carole, **#307** Wilderness Patrol, ranger Scott & woodsman Red, **#351** Mountain Climbers, climbers Mike and Jan, **#350** Rescue Team, Mike & Susan, **#308** Super Speed Racer, driver Buzz, **#356** Cycle Racing Team, racer, **#312** North Woods Trailblazer, explorer Brad & guide Hawk, and **#303** Emergency Rescue Truck, rescuer Tom.
Loose figures. **$3.00 each.**
MOC. **$8.00 – $15.00 each.**

1980 – 1982 Each case contained one of 11 different figures on a newly designed full-color blister pack. This picture is of a store display and shows only 11 of 28 different figures sold during this period. Six new figures were introduced, Space Commander, Highway Trooper, Supersonic Pilot, X-Ray Woman, X-Ray Man Clawtron, and Opticon.
Loose figures. **$3.00.**
Alien space figures can go for as much as **$15.00 each.**
MOC. **$8.00 – $15.00.**

#394 Adventure Figure Assortment. 1983 – 1984. Three figures on each blister pack with six different blister packs. Each figure had the same name as the set it was sold with; the new figures' names are Alpha Pilot and Brainoid.
Loose figures. **$3.00.**
Alien space figures can go for as much as **$15.00 each.**
MOC. **$20.00 – $25.00.**

#399 Adventure Figure Assortment. 1983 – 1984 Each case contained one of 32 different figures sold during this period.
Loose figures. **$3.00.**
Alien space figures can go for as much as **$15.00 each.**
MOC. **$15.00 – $20.00.**

#418 Freddy Bear. 1976 – 1980. Cuddly plush bear with attached bib. **$10.00.**

#415 Music Box Owl. 1973 – 1977. Plays Schubert's "Cradle Song." Felt eyes and nose. Plush front, back and ears colored twill. **$10.00.**

#423 Jumping Jack Scare-crow. 1979 – 1980. Jumping Jack hangs on crib or playpen. Ring attached to string attracts baby's eye. When pulled, arms and legs move up-down and Jack makes a squeak sound as eyes look left and right. **$10.00.**

#435 Happy Apple. 1973 – 1978. Roly Poly chime toy that floats. Has a long stem. Soft leaves for teething. **$6.00.**

1979 – 1984. Stem was made much smaller. **$3.00.**

#448 Mini Copter. 1971 – 1984. Blue litho copter with whirlybird motion. Rotor spins to whirling sound as rear stabilizer turns. **$10.00.**

#450 Music Box Bear. 1981 – 1983. Hangs on crib or playpen with adjustable plastic strap. Plays Schubert's "Cradle Song" when ring is pulled. **$10.00.**

#460 Movie Viewer and Cartridge. 1973 – 1985. Viewer and one cartridge #475 "Lonesome Ghost." **$8.00.**

#460A Movie Viewer and Cartridge, Walt Disney, 1980. Viewer and one cartridge. The viewer is white and has the same litho as the cartridge. Cartridge is "The Black Hole." **$15.00 each.**

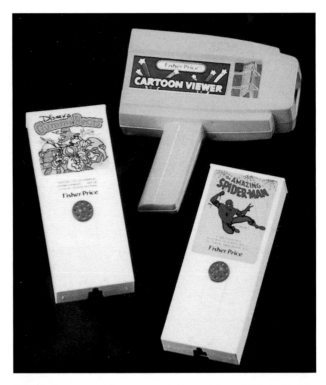

#460 Cartoon Viewer and Cartridge. 1986. Newly designed viewer with cartridge, viewer plastic is yellow, and litho is blue with streaking stars. Came with the cartridge "Gummi Bears." **$10.00.**

#462 Viewer Cartridge, Walt Disney. 1979 – 1986. "The Rescuers." **$6.00.**

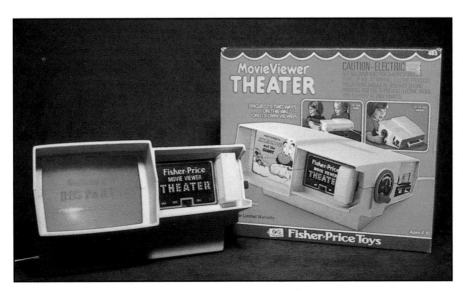

#463 Movie Viewer Theater. 1977 – 1986. Movie theater works two ways, on a private viewing screen or on a wall. Just slip in any of the interchangeable cartridges, focus, and turn crank on side for fast, slow or backward motion. Includes movie cartridge "Mickey Mouse and the Giant." **$20.00.**

#464 Pocket Camera. 1974 – 1990. Push button, flash cube turns, click-click sound. Twenty-seven pictures of "A Trip To The Zoo." **$5.00.**
1991. Same basic camera with new litho of chicken and stars on flash cube. **$5.00.**

#465 Movie Viewer Starter Kit. 1973 – 1985. Viewer and one cartridge, "On My Way to Sesame Street." **$8.00.**
1986 – 1987 Viewer and one cartridge, **#485** "Snoopy Meets the Red Baron." **$8.00.**

Viewer Cartridges #467 – 499
#467 1973 – 1979. Donald Duck's Toy Train. **$6.00.**
#469 Warner Bros. 1979 – 1987. Sylvester & Tweety. **$6.00.**
#470 Walt Disney. 1973 – 1978. Fox and Hound. **$6.00.**
#471 United Artists. 1973 – 1978. The Pink Panther. **$6.00.**
#472 Peanuts. 1986 – 1987. Snoopy's Big Party. **$6.00.**
#473 Peanuts. 1986 – 1987. Snoopy Tennis Classic, white cartridge. **$6.00.**
#474 Walt Disney. 1973 – 1978. Mickey Mouse and the Giant. **$6.00.**
#475 Walt Disney. 1973 – 1978. Lonesome Ghosts. **$6.00.**
#476 Walt Disney. 1973 – 1979. Pinocchio. **$6.00.**
  1986 – 1987 White cartridge. **$6.00.**
#477 Walt Disney. 1973 – 1979. Cinderella, Fairy God-mother and Prince Charming. **$6.00.**
#478 Walt Disney. 1973 – 1979. Dumbo the Flying Ele-phant and Dumbo Makes The Big Top. **$6.00.**
#479 Walt Disney. 1973 – 1979 Snow White Meets the Seven Dwarfs and Snow White the Dwarfs' Dilemma. **$6.00.**
  1986 – 1987 White cartridge. **$6.00.**
#480 Walt Disney. 1973 – 1979. Bambi Falls in Love & Bambi and His Friends. **$6.00.**

#481 Walt Disney. 1973 – 1979. Three Little Pigs. **$6.00.**

#482 Walt Disney. 1973 – 1979. Good Scouts. **$6.00.**

#482 1982 – 1987. Snoopy meets the Red Baron. Cartridge came in white or yellow plastic. **$6.00.**

#483 Walt Disney. 1973 – 1979. Mary Poppins. **$6.00.**

#483 Walt Disney. 1979 – 1987. Winnie the Pooh and The Blustery Day. **$6.00.**

#484 Walt Disney. 1979 – 1985. Winnie the Pooh and Tigger Too. **$8.00.**

#484 Dates unknown. Viewer and cartridge Winnie the Pooh Honey Tree. **$10.00.** No picture is available of this set.

#485 Sesame Street. 1973 – 1979. On Our Way to Sesame Street. **$6.00.**

#486 Sesame Street. 1973 – 1979. Numbers. **$6.00,** **1986 – 1987** White cartridge. **$6.00.**

#487 Sesame Street. 1973 – 1979. Sizes. **$6.00.**

#488 Sesame Street. 1973 – 1979. Shapes. **$6.00.**

#488 Peanuts. 1982 – 1987. Joe Cool on Campus, white cartridge. **$6.00.**

#489 Sesame Street. 1973 – 1979. Alphabet. **$6.00,** **1986 – 1987** White cartridge. **$6.00.**

#490 Walt Disney. 1974 – 1979. Goofy's Glider. **$6.00.**

#491 Walt Disney. 1974 – 1979. Mickey's Trailer. **$6.00.**

#492 Walt Disney. 1974 – 1979. Robin Hood. **$6.00.**

#492 Peanut's. 1982 – 1987. Snoopy to the Rescue. **$6.00.**

#493 Walt Disney. 1974 – 1979. Bear Trouble and The Fox and The Hound. **$6.00.**

#493 Peanut's. 1982 – 1987. Peppermint Patty on Ice. **$6.00.**

#494 Walt Disney. 1974 – 1979. Flight Into Space. **$6.00.**

#494 Peanut's. 1982 – 1985. It's A Hit Charlie Brown. **$6.00.**

#495 Walt Disney. 1974 – 1979. Featuring Pluto, Bone Trouble. **$6.00.**

#495 Movie Viewer Starter Kit. **1982 – 1987.** Viewer and cartridge, Snoopy Meets the Red Baron. **$8.00.**

#496 Warner Bros. 1974 – 1979. Bugs Bunny in the Lions Den. **$6.00.**

#497 Warner Bros. 1979 – 1987. Road Runner in Zipping Along. **$6.00.**

#498 Sesame Street. 1979 – 1987. Big Bird's Birthday Party. **$6.00.**

#499 Sesame Street. 1986 – 1987. Cookie Monster in the Kitchen. **$6.00.**

#500 Pick-up and Peek Puzzles.
Note: #502, 503, 507, 508, 510 & 516 have stand-up play features.

#476 Cookie Pig. 1966 – 1970. Makes oink-oink sound and tail spins around. **$50.00.**

#501 Barn. 1972 – 1984. Thirteen pieces. Resembles #915 Play Family Farm. **$10.00.**

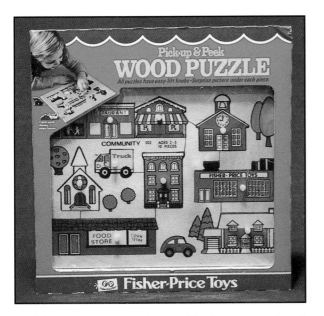

#502 Community. 1972 – 1978. Ten pieces. Small town resembles East Aurora, N.Y. **$10.00.**

#503 Occupations. 1972 – 1976. Eight pieces. Fireman, astronaut, mom, cowboy, police officer, ballerina, nurse, construction man. **$10.00.**

#504 Cap'n Crunch and crew. 1971 only. Good ship Guppy and crew; very rare. **$30.00.**

#504 Castle. 1984 only. Twelve pieces. Castle with horse and knight. **$15.00.**

#505 Cap'n Crunch. 1971 only. Cap'n Crunch. Very rare. **$30.00.**

#506 Bear and Cubs. 1972 – 1984. Ten pieces. Mama bear, babies. **$10.00.**

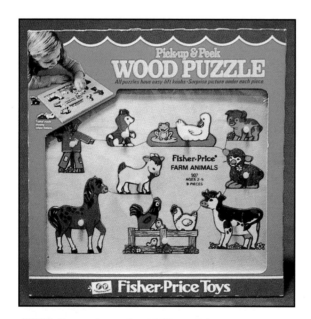

#507 Farm Animals. 1972 – 1984. Nine pieces. Scarecrow, dog, duck, pig, goat, lamb, horse, chickens, and cow. **$10.00.**

#508 Vehicles. 1972 – 1984. Eight pieces. Plane, boat, sailboat, truck, car, and three-piece train. **$10.00.**

Not pictured
#509 Children Around the World. 1972 only. Eight pieces. Eskimo, Japanese, Mexican, African, Dutch, Hawaiian, American Indian, and Scottish children. **$10.00.**

#510 Nursery Rhymes. 1972 – 1981. Six pieces. Humpty Dumpty, Three Men In A Tub, Jack and Jill, Little Boy Blue, and Hey Diddle-Diddle. **$15.00.**

#511 Dog and Puppies. 1972 – 1984. Eight pieces. Dog and two puppies. **$10.00.**

#512 Horse and Colt. 1972 – 1973. Horse and colt; rare. **$15.00.**

#513 House. 1972 – 1978. Twelve pieces. Play Family house and Lucky. **$10.00.**

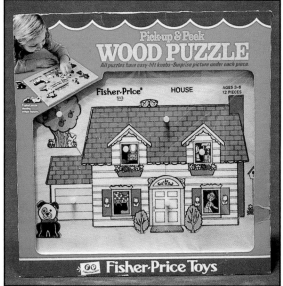

#514 Merry-Go-Round. 1972 – 1976. Twelve pieces. Resembles #111 Play Family Merry-Go-Round. **$15.00.**

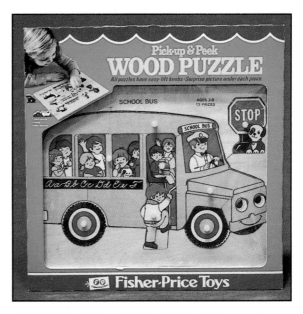

#515 School Bus. 1973 – 1984. Thirteen pieces. Similar to #192 Play Family Bus. **$10.00.**

#516 Circus. 1973 – 1976. Eight pieces. Elephant, ring master, lion tamer, lion, horse, clown, bear, and balloon vendor. **$10.00.**

#519 Animal Friends. 1977 – 1984. Eight pieces. Doe, ground hog, bear, squirrel, rabbit, raccoon, wood chuck, and skunk. **$10.00.**

Not pictured

#517 House Boat. 1977 – 1978. Twelve pieces. Similar to Play Family Boat; rare. **$20.00.**

#518 Tree House. 1977 – 1978. Thirteen pieces. Tree house with boy climbing ladder and one on swing. Rare. **$10.00.**

#520 Three Little Pigs. 1979 – 1984. Twelve pieces. **$15.00.**

#521 Old Woman Who Lived in a Shoe. 1979 – 1981. Thirteen pieces. Shoe with old lady and kids. **$15.00.**

#522 Colors. 1980 – 1984. Five pieces. Similar to Play Family School with sun, tree, and pumpkin. **$10.00.**

#523 Animals and their Babies. 1982 – 1984. Eight pieces. Eight different animals and babies. **$10.00.**

Action Model Kits

Kit includes plastic parts, permanently attached screws, screw key, stick-on decals, and instructions.

#526 Action Model Kit F-15 Eagle. 1984 – 1985. Camouflaged turbo jet with opening canopy. **$10.00.**

#527 Action Model Kit Light Speed Fighter. 1984 – 1985. Rotating flight station detaches with accessible cockpit. **$10.00.**

#528 Action Model Kit Ford EXP. 1984 – 1985. "Hot Stuff" car has lift-up body with support bar, rubber tires, and a rear spoiler. **$10.00.**

#529 Action Model Kit Chevy Road Rebel 4X4. 1984 – 1985. Truck has working tailgate, heavy duty bumpers, and roll bar with lights. **$15.00.**

#530 Action Model Kit "Huey Cobra" 1984 – 1985. Copter has lift-up canopy and rotating blades. **$15.00.**

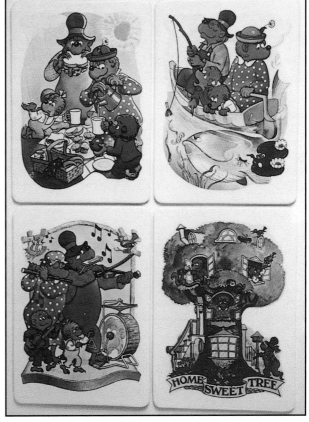

#537 Berenstain Bears, S & J Berenstain. 1982 only. Tree House, eight masonite pieces and plastic tray. **$10.00.**

#538 Berenstain Bears, S & J Berenstain. 1982 only. Family Band, six masonite pieces and plastic tray. **$10.00.**

#539 Berenstain Bears, S & J Berenstain. 1982 only. Perfect Picnic Spot, seven masonite pieces and plastic tray. **$10.00.**

#540 Berenstain Bears, S & J Berenstain. 1982 only. Go Fishing, seven masonite pieces and plastic tray. **$10.00.**

#541 1981 – 1982. Kermit the Frog, six masonite pieces and plastic tray. **$10.00.**

#542 1981 – 1982. Miss Piggy, eight masonite pieces and plastic tray. **$10.00.**

#543 1981 – 1982. Miss Piggy, seven masonite pieces and plastic tray. **$10.00.**

#544 1981 – 1982. Balloon Ride, nine masonite pieces and plastic tray. **$10.00.**

#545 1981 – 1982. The Photographer, eight masonite pieces and plastic tray. **$10.00.**

#546 1981 – 1982. Sidekick, nine masonite pieces and plastic tray. **$10.00.**

#547 1981 – 1982. The Muppets, eight masonite pieces and plastic tray. **$10.00.**

#548 1981 – 1982. The Electric Mayhem, nine masonite pieces and plastic tray. **$10.00.**

Hardboard Puzzles

#551 Fruit & Shapes. 1974 – 1975. Six pieces. **$10.00.**

#552 Nature. 1974 – 1975. Six pieces. **$15.00.**

#553 Sheep & Lambs. 1974 – 1975. Six pieces. **$10.00.**

#554 Owl & Babies. 1974 – 1975. Six pieces. **$10.00.**

#555 Rabbit & Bunnies. 1974 – 1975. Six pieces. **$10.00.**

#556 Puppy. 1974 – 1975. Nine pieces. **$10.00.**

#557 City. 1974 – 1975. Twelve pieces. **$10.00.**

#558 Jack and Jill. 1974 – 1975. Thirteen pieces. **$10.00.**

#559 Horse. 1974 – 1975. Ten pieces. **$10.00.**

#560 Cow. 1974 – 1975. Ten pieces. **$10.00.**

#561 Fire Engine. 1974 – 1975. Twelve pieces. **$10.00.**

#562 Jet Transport. 1974. Ten pieces. **$10.00.**

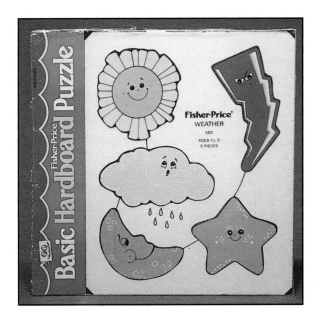

#563 Weather, Hardboard Puzzle. 1975. Five pieces. **$10.00.**

#564 Farm, Hardboard Puzzle. 1975. Five pieces. **$10.00.**

Not pictured
#565 Robins In Nest, Hardboard Puzzle. 1975. Six pieces. **$10.00.**

#566 Duck and Ducklings, Hardboard Puzzle. 1975. Six pieces. **$10.00.**

#567 Cat and Kittens, Hardboard Puzzle. 1975. Six pieces. **$10.00.**

#568 Bears, Hardboard Puzzle. 1975. Eight pieces. **$10.00.**

#569 Airport, Hardboard Puzzle. 1975. Eleven pieces. **$10.00.**

#570 Goldilocks, Hardboard Puzzle. 1975. Twelve pieces. **$10.00.**

#571 Elephant, Hardboard Puzzle. 1975. Ten pieces. **$10.00.**

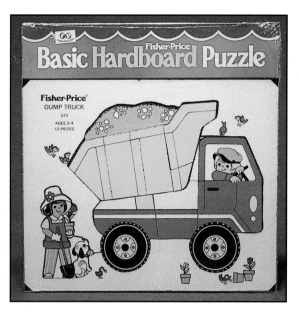

#573 Dump Truck, Hardboard Puzzle. 1975. Twelve pieces. **$10.00.**

Not pictured

#572 Raccoon, Hardboard Puzzle. 1975. Ten pieces. **$10.00.**

#574 Police Car, Hardboard Puzzle. 1975. Ten pieces. **$10.00.**

#605 Woodsey Mayor Goodgrub Mole. 1981 – 1982. "Mayor Goodgrub's Very Important Day" 32-page book and Mayor Goodgrub figure. **$20.00.**

#606 Woodsey Bramble Beaver. 1981 – 1982. "Bramble Beaver's Bright Idea" 32-page book and Bramble Beaver figure. **$20.00.**

#607 Woodsey Very Blue Bird. 1981 – 1982. "The Seasons With Very Blue Bird" 32-page book and Very Blue Bird figure with pouch. **$20.00.**

#617 Prancy Pony. 1965 – 1970. Prancing up and down motion on big polyethylene balloon wheels. Makes clippity-clop, clippity-clop sound. Head and tail mounted on springs. **$30.00.**

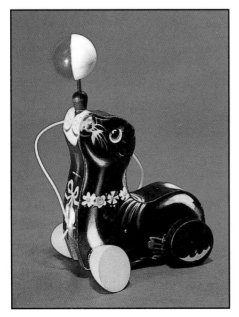

#621 Suzie Seal. 1965 – 1966. Black litho seal with bell on her chest and a ball on her nose. **$40.00.**

#623 Suzie Seal. 1964 – 1965. Red plastic Suzie has a spring-mounted umbrella on her nose and a bell that rings on her chest. **$55.00.**

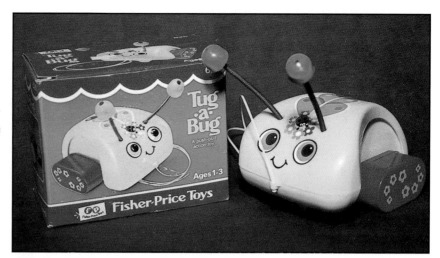

#628 Tug-A-Bug. 1975 – 1977. All-plastic feet flip flop, antennae mounted on springs. **$5.00.**

#634 Drummer Boy. 1967 – 1969. Drummer beats hollow drum. Mallets mounted on springs. Wood drummer on plastic base. This was the last toy made with moving arms until the 1991 ToyFest "Teddy Bear Parade." **$50.00.**

Note: The drummer boy's face is that of Eric Smith, son of John Smith, former art director, John did most of the art work on the Little People playset lithos. This image was also used on the #112, #784, and #919.

#635 Air Lift Copter. 1983 – 1984. Blue and white copter with orange cage and tall green pilot. **$6.00.**

1985. Number changed (see #2449)

#636 Farm Fun. 1983 – 1984. Tractor with cart, red rooster, dog, and farmer. **$4.00.** (See #2448)

#637 Milk Carrier. 1966 – 1985. Yellow plastic carrier with four white bottles, one brown, and one orange. **$15.00.**

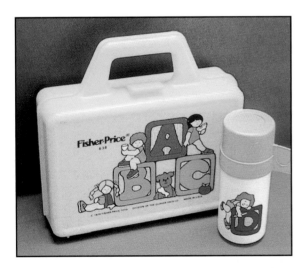

#638 Play Lunch Box. 1980 – 1985. Lunch box with A, B, C blocks printed on it. Four ounce thermos with "D" on it. **$8.00.**

#642 Bob-Along Bear. 1979 – 1984. Little bear's arms twirl and colored beads rattle inside his wheels. **$10.00.**

#643 Toot-Toot Engine. 1964 – 1987. Red litho train with four blue wood wheels and chug-chug sound. In the first year of production, the number of the toy was beside the front wheels. After that it was moved to just above the rear wheels. **$20.00.**

The changes in the last two versions were from wood wheels on front and plastic on the rear to all four wheels being made of plastic. Either of these versions. **$5.00.**

Of the four versions of this toy, the wood wheeled with the number beside the front wheel is one of the hardest to find.

#644 Tag-Along Turtle. 1978 – 1986. Salty turtle wags tail, rolls along on flipper-like feet, and makes ratchet sound. **$5.00.**

1992 Reissued (see #2254)

#656 Play Family Little Riders. 1977 – 1990. Seven piece set. Coaster with movable steering wheel, jet, riding horse, train engine, tricycle, boy and girl figures of any color and style. **$6.00.**
Note: The descriptions of the figures and pieces are as pictured in 1977 catalogs and boxes. The figures and pieces could be in any color combination.

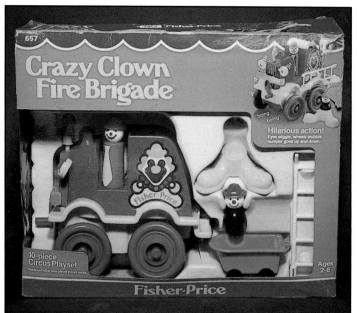

#657 Crazy Clown Fire Brigade. 1983 – 1984. Comical fire truck with 10 interchangeable pieces. Truck makes bongs sound. Headlights and wheels wobble, radiator cap and bumper move up and down. Crank turns on front making ratchet sound. Two clown firefighters with red hats, short/black and tall/blue. The tall clown's tie can be either yellow or white, barrel, "funny feet," two fire hoses also double as shower piece, bathtub on wheels, and two ladders that hook together. **$50.00.**

#659 Puzzle Puppy. 1976 – 1981. Eight pieces. Take apart, put together dog. **$10.00.**
Note; This is a life-size verison of the Little People Lucky dog. Everyone should have at least one.

#663 Play Family Set. 1966 – 1970. These figures were all wood sold in a rectangular shaped box. Green dad with heat stamped hair, blue mom with white hair, red girl with blonde hair, green girl with red hair, red boy with yellow cowboy hat, blue boy with red cap, and either a black straight bodied or tan regular dog.
Set unopened with black dog. **$120.00.**
Set unopened with tan dog. **$170.00.**
Per wood figure, not including the brown dog. **$3.00.** Tan dog. **$30.00.**

1971 – 1974. Now on blister card and dog was always black. These figures were made with plastic heads and wood bodies. **$20.00.**
Note: The above listed figures could have come in any color combination.

1974 – 1990. Figures are now all plastic and could have come in any color. **$10.00.**
This price is for all common plastic figures. **$1.50.**

#666 Creative Blocks. 1978 – 1990. Fourteen colored plastic blocks, six triangular, four round, four square, and four plastic dowel rods. **$10.00.**

#675 Circus Clowns. 1984 – 1990. The figures are listed below as pictured in the catalogs. Price for blister card unopened. **$15.00.** Price per figure. **$2.00.**

1984 – 1988 Orange clown with black western hat, green clown with blue top hat, and purple clown with yellow cone hat.

1989 – 1990 Orange clown with back western hat, green clown with blue top hat, and red clown with yellow cone hat.

#676 Westerners. 1984 – 1990. Green cowboy with mustache and white hat, red Indian with white headdress and blue marking, and tall black gambler. Price for blister card unopened **$15.00.** Price per figure. **$2.00.**

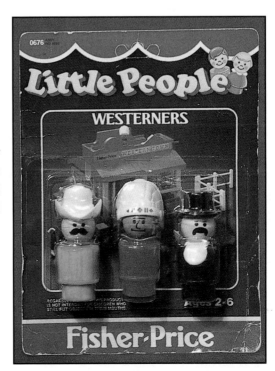

#677 Picnic Basket. 1975 – 1979. Plastic picnic basket, plate, spoon, bear-shaped bottle with cup, and cotton tablecloth. **$30.00.**

#677 Farm Family. 1984 – 1983. The figures are listed below as pictured in the catalogs. Price for blister card unopened. **$15.00.** Price per plastic figure. **$1.00.**

1984 – 1988. Green farmer with white cowboy hat, yellow girl with brown hair, and red mom with yellow hair.

1989 – 1990. Green farmer with white cowboy hat, blue girl with yellow hair, and red mom with yellow hair.

#678 Jetport Crew. 1984 – 1993. The figures are listed below as pictured in the catalogs. Price for blister card unopened. **$15.00.** Price per figure. **$2.00.**

1984 – 1988. White pilot with tan body and blue hat, tan stewardess with blue hat, and black pilot with blue body and hat.

1989 – 1990. White pilot with green body and hat, light blue stewardess with hat, and black pilot with dark blue body and hat.
Note: The stewardess could also be dark blue and is a rare find. Unopened blister card. **$30.00.**

#679 *Garage Squad. 1984 – 1990.* The figures are listed below as pictured in the catalogs. Price for blister card unopened. **$15.00.** Price per figure. **$1.50.**

1984 – 1988. Figures are white man, tan body with silver hard hat, and yellow scarf; black man, green body, yellow hard hat, and white scarf; and white man, blue body with orange hard hat, and orange scarf.

1989 – 1990. Figures are white man, green body, yellow hard hat, and yellow scarf; black man, light blue body, orange hard hat, and orange scarf; and white man, dark blue body, orange hard hat, and orange scarf.

#684 Little Lamb. 1964 – 1965. Up and down motion on yellow polyethylene balloon wheels, metal bell rings and tail swings when toy is pulled. **$50.00.**

#685 Car and Boat. 1968 – 1969. Five piece set. Plastic white and red car with hook and white or red trailer, white and red or white and blue plastic boat with two holes on bottom, yellow straight bodied boy with red or blue cap, and dog with blue or red ribless collar. **$65.00.** **Note:** MIB can sell for as much as **$130.00.**

#686 Car & Camper. 1968 – 1970. Five piece set. Plastic white and red car with hook and white or red trailer, wood camper, yellow straight bodied boy with red or white cap, and dog with blue or red ribless collar. **$65.00.** **Note:** MIB can sell for as much as **$130.00.** The 1968 version of the car has a metal rivet on the bottom and the 1969+ versions do not.

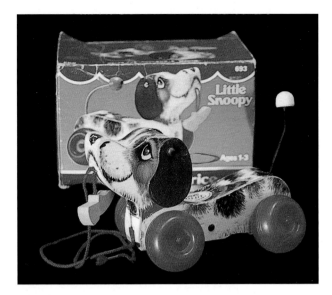

#693 Little Snoopy. 1966 – 1989. Yip-yip sound produced when pulled and has a wooden body with wooden shoe hanging from mouth. Has a spring-attached tail tipped with wood bead. **$3.00.**

1984 – 1989. Later made in all plastic. **$2.00.**

1990. Number changed (see #2034)

#694 Suzie Seal. 1979 – 1980. Brown seal with yellow and white plastic ball attached to a spring on her nose. This was the last wooden pull toy introduced. **$15.00.**
Note: This was the last wooden pull toy introduced as a regular toy. However, it was not the last wooden toy made of Ponderosa pine at the plant: the #6588 was.

#695 Lady Bug. 1982 – 1984. Plastic lady bug with two-piece body waddles along to ratchet sound, and antennae sway to and fro. **$5.00.**

#699 1981 – 1985. Six Farm and Circus Animals, each one on its own blister card. Cow, horse, lion, monkey, bear, and giraffe. MOC. **$8.00 each.**

#700 Art Kit. 1981 – 1983. Plastic storage case with 16 crayons; crayon sharpener; five colored chalks, red, orange, yellow, green, blue; four watercolors, red, blue, yellow, green; tray with paintbrush; scissors; 6" ruler; three stencils, circle, square, and triangle; six sheets construction paper; glue; two magnets; and idea book. **$15.00.**

#701 Printer's Kit. 1981 – 1984. Plastic case with 78 printing pieces, composing frame, ink pad, bottle of blue ink, construction paper, and idea book. **$15.00.**

Note: Girl on right is author's daughter Jenna, 13, and friend Jen, 13.

#702 Button-Ups. 1981 – 1983. Fifty-eight pieces consisting of 30 foam and fabric pieces in varying shapes and 28 plastic buttons. Shapes and buttons in four colors, red, yellow, blue, and green. **$10.00.**

#703 Crazy Clay Characters. 1981 – 1983. Thirty-two plastic pieces. Hands, feet, hats, facial features, and other accessory pieces. Three piece plastic storage container and ¾ lb. blue stay-soft clay. This price is for the complete set, **$30.00.**

#704 Wood Airplane Kit. 1982 – 1985. Wooden single engine plane with plastic landing strut, wheels, propeller, and decals. Came with pre-cut wood, glue, sandpaper, and instructions. MIB, **$25.00.** Assembled, **$8.00.**

#705 Mini Snowmobile. 1971 – 1973. Snowmobile with detachable sled and matching runners. Runners came in either black or red. Two aqua blue wood figures boy with a red hat, girl with red hair, and black dog. **$45.00.**

#705 Wood Sailboat Kit. 1982 – 1985. Catamaran sailboat with plastic rudder, mast, boom, nylon sail, and decals. Came with pre-cut wood, glue, sandpaper, and instructions. Assembled, **$8.00.** MIB, **$25.00.**

#706 Wood Bird Feeder Kit. 1982 – 1985. Bird feeder with two clear plastic windows, cord for hanging, and plastic cap for filler hole on top. Assembled, **$10.00.** MIB, **$25.00.**

Not pictured
#707 Easy-Etch Print Maker Kit. 1982 only. Print making kit combines drawing, tracing, printing, etching, and coloring. Came with four watercolor pencils, wipe-off tissues, sponge, 12 acetate sheets, 12 sheets of paper, idea sheet, reusable storage tray, and instructions. **$25.00.**

#708 Sunshine Mobile Butterflies. 1982 – 1984. Thirty-one piece kit with six clear plastic butterflies, one ring for hanging, 4⅜ oz. tubs liquid Stay-Bright Color, 20 T-end connectors. Makes a 20" high mobile. Assembled, **$5.00.** MIB, **$25.00.**

#709 Sunshine Mobile Airplanes and Balloons. 1982 – 1984. **$25.00.** (Same as **#708**)

Not pictured
#710 Activity Calendar. 1983 – 1985. Two boards with four wipe-off surfaces, lace to connect the boards, 23 reusable vinyl stickers, 15 holiday, four weather, four season, and adhesive-backed magnet. **$10.00.**

#711 Cry Baby Bear. 1967 – 1969. Sad-eyed baby bear's head moves up and down when pulled, makes crying sound. Wood body and plastic head. **$30.00.**

#712 Creative Clips. 1983 – 1984. Three plastic clips, Sailboat, Rainbow, and Ice Cream Sundae, to make book markers, refrigerator magnets or paper clips. Three Stay-Bright colors, red, white, and blue, three magnets, and instructions. Assembled, **$8.00.** MIB, **$25.00.**

Toy and photo courtesy of Linda Meunier.

#715 Ducky Flip-Flap. 1964 – 1965. Duck with 4" long flexible flipper-feet. Waddles side to side making a quack-quack sound. 21" push stick. **$65.00.**

#715 Weaving Loom. 1983 – 1986. Eight piece plastic loom with alphabetized pegs, three weaving shuttles, comb, plastic needle, enough yarn to make purse or scarf, and instructions. **$15.00.**

#716 Play Family Farm Tractor and Cart. 1969 – 1972. Five piece set. Blue boy farmer/red hat, tractor, cart, chicken, and rooster. MIB, **$30.00.** As a set with wood figures. **$8.00.**

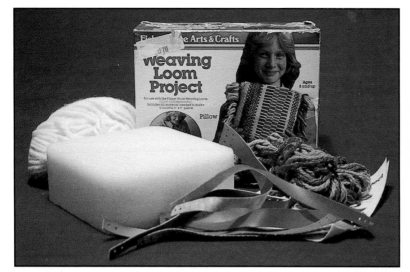

#716 Weaving Loom Project "Pillow" 1983 – 1985. Foam pillow insert 9" x 9", yarn, plastic needle, instructions. **$5.00.**

#717 Weaving Loom Project "Tote Bag." 1983 – 1985. Yarn, plastic needle, vinyl pieces, and instruction to make an 8½" x 9" bag. **$5.00.**

#718 Tow Truck and Car. 1969 – 1970. Tow truck driver bounces and flasher turns, has wood base and wheels. Plastic single passenger car and straight bodied yellow boy with white or blue cap. MIB. **$75.00.** Truck, car, and figure. **$30.00.**
Note: It has been said that the hook on the tow truck was eliminated in 1970 due to safety standards but I have never seen one MIB like this. I have seen played-with tow trucks with no hooks.

Not pictured
#718 Weaving Loom Project "Wall Organizer." 1984 – 1985. Makes a 7¼" x 17" organizer, using yarn, two sticks, and instructions. **$5.00.**

#719 Cuddly Cub. 1973 – 1977. Head turns and bear chimes when rocked. Lift-up bib has pocket. **$5.00.**

#720 Fisher-Price Fire Engine. 1968 – 1972. With wooden head driver and fireman. 12" hose, extension ladder. Bell rings as toy is pulled. The litho on both sides has "FP Fire Engine." **$10.00.**

1973 – 1979. The litho on both sides now says "Fisher-Price Fire Engine." Also the figures can be either wood and plastic or all plastic and the driver's head is plastic. **$8.00.**

#721 Sesame Street Clay Pals. 1984 only. Twenty-one colorful plastic pieces. Make Big Bird, Grover or Cookie Monster with arms, legs, and heads for each character, cowboy hat, chief's hat, beanie with spinning propeller, five-point star, working skateboard, and one pound of blue and yellow clay. **$20.00.**

#724 Jolly Jalopy. 1965 only. Circus clown roadster with wobbling motion, rounded eyes, and black outlined mouth. Head mounted on spring. Makes putt-putt engine sound. Big red polyethylene balloon tires. **$15.00.**

1966 – 1978. Circus clown's eyes and mouth had a make-over. The eyes are now a half circle shape and the mouth outlined in black and red. **$8.00.**

The third Jolly Jalopy pictured we have very little information on other than their existence. It was made either winter of 1964 – 1965 or winter of 1965 – 1966. If you note, his eyes are in a star shape but the rest of the toy is the same as the 1965 one. What would happen often is the same as the **#643** Toot-Toot. It was put into production but months into it Fisher-Price would decide to make a few changes for whatever reason.

#725 Play Family Bath/Utility Room Set. 1972 – 1978. Twelve piece set. Bathtub, vanity sink, toilet, bathroom scale, washer, dryer, chair and sewing machine; green dad, heat stamped hair, blue mom, blonde hair, red boy, heat stamped hair, and blue girl, blonde hair. Price is for set unopened. **$75.00.** Loose set, **$30.00.**
Note: The descriptions of the figures are as pictured in 1972 catalogs and boxes. The figures and pieces could be in any color combination.

#726 Play Family House Patio Set. 1970 – 1973. Eleven piece set. Wading pool with imprint, table with flower-imprinted umbrella and four chairs, grill. All-wood green dad, heat stamped hair, blue mom, blonde hair, blue girl, blonde hair, and orange boy, heat stamped hair. Price is for set unopened. **$75.00.** Loose set, **$30.00.**
Note: The descriptions of the figures are as pictured in 1972 catalogs and boxes. The figures and pieces could be in any color combination.

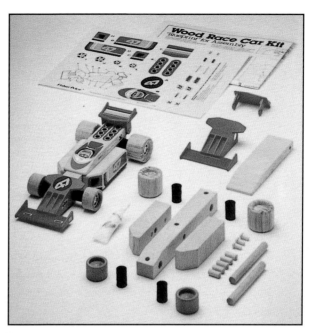

#726 Wood Racer Kit. 1983 – 1985. Indy racer with four wood wheels, two plastic spoilers, and sheet of decals. Assembled, **$8.00.** MIB, **$25.00.**

#727 Little Lace-Ups Horse. 1981 – 1985. Plastic shapes with holes to be laced up with 34" red and white lace. **$5.00.**

#728 Little Lace-Ups Bear. 1981 – 1985. Same as #727. **$5.00.**

#729 Little Lace-Ups Bunny. 1981 – 1985. Same as #727. **$5.00.**

#728 Pound and Saw Bench. 1966 – 1967. Safety saw pushed back and forth across bench makes realistic sawing sound. Hammer for pounding wooden nail makes squeak-squeak sound when struck. Plastic hammer head on a wooden handle and saw with plastic handle. **$25.00.**

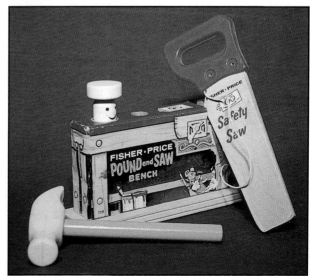

#728 Play Family House Decorator Set. 1970 – 1972. Thirteen piece set. This set has either two or three different colors of furniture, brown, orange, or yellow on each blister card. Two twins and one double bed, two wing chairs, love seat, coffee table, TV-stereo, checkered litho game table; all-wood figures; blue mom, blonde hair, green dad, heat stamped hair, blue girl, blonde hair, and orange boy, heat stamped hair. Price is for set unopened. **$125.00.** Loose set, **$35.00.**

Note: The descriptions of the figures are as pictured in 1970 catalogs and boxes. The figures could be in any color combination.

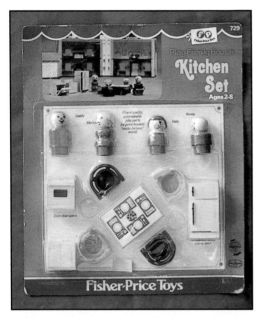

#729 Play Family House Kitchen Set. 1970 – 1975. Twelve piece set. Lime green table with litho flower centerpiece, four captains chairs, two lime green and two brown, yellow sink, stove with or without litho top, refrigerator; wood blue mom with blonde hair, green dad with heat stamped hair, orange boy with heat stamped hair, and blue girl with blonde hair. Price is for set unopened. **$75.00.** Loose set, **$30.00.**

Note: The descriptions of the figures are as pictured in 1970 catalogs and boxes. The figures could be in any color combination.

#732 Happy Hauler 1968 – 1970. Wood garden tractor with plastic cart. Makes putt-putt sound, and driver sways side to side. **$35.00.**

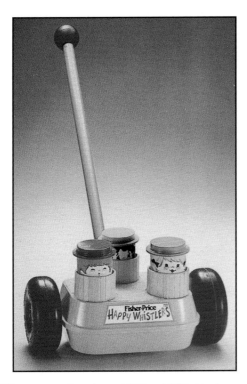

#734 Teddy Zilo. 1964. Jovial brown bear, pivoting xylophone with three keys. Litho did not have a band coat nor the word "Teddy" on his hat. **$65.00.**

#732 Happy Whistlers. 1977 – 1979. Push or pull, three comical children peek up and down and make different whistling sounds. **$15.00.**

1965 – 1966 New litho design. Bear is wearing a band coat and the word "Teddy" is on his hat. **$45.00.**

#736 Humpty Dumpty. 1972 – 1979. All-plastic pull toy rocks back and forth as hands spin around, makes jabbering sound when pulled. **$4.00.**
Note: The hat came in either yellow or the harder-to-find color, red.

#737 Simple Stitch Quilting "Pot Holders." 1984 – 1985. Material for apple, ice cream sundae, and cheeseburger designs, four-piece plastic frame, die-cut pre-punched fabric pieces. yarn, polyester batting, blunt tapestry needle, and instructions. **$6.00.**

#741 Teddy Zilo. 1967 only. Happy Teddy with pivoting xylophone and three steel keys. **$45.00.**

#739 Simple Stitch Quilting "Tote Bag." 1984 – 1985. Makes Tote Bag with roller skate design. Same supplies as #737. **$6.00.**

#741 Starting Stitchery "Girl with Flowers." 1981 – 1984. Plastic grid with holes and printed design, six colors of yarn, green, red, orange, light blue, yellow, and dark blue, snap-in frame, two plastic needles, and instructions. **$6.00.**

#742 Starting Stitchery "Butterfly." 1981 – 1986. Same supplies as #741. **$6.00.**
Note: Girl in photo is author's daughter, Dinah, age 8.

Not pictured
#743 Starting Stitchery "Strawberries." 1981 – 1984. Same supplies as #741. **$6.00.**

#744 Starting Stitchery "Kitten." 1982 – 1984. Same supplies as #741. **$6.00.**

#745 Creative Stamper Caddy "Space Scenes." 1984 – 1986. Blue plastic caddy, six stamps w/handles, 10 crayons and sharpener, decal sheet, ink pad with lid, and idea book. **$15.00.** (See also #5526)

#746 Creative Stamper Caddy "Jungle Scenes." 1984 – 1986. Orange plastic caddy with the same parts as #745. **$15.00.** Space Scenes also pictured.

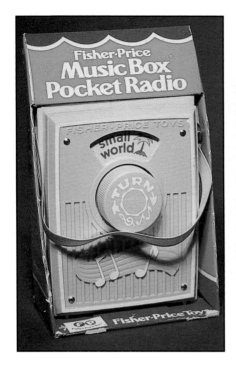

#746 "It's A Small World" Pocket Radio. 1977 – 1978. Wood case with plastic face. **$25.00.**

#747 Chatter Telephone. 1962 – 1967. Phone with wooden wheels and base makes chatter sound when pulled and realistic ringing sound when dialed. **$30.00.**

1968 – 1985 Plastic wheels and wooden base. **$4.00.**

1986 – 1990 The phone base was made of plastic and the litho was redesigned. The sides of the phone no longer have "F-P," but now read "Fisher-Price." **$4.00.**

#748 Color With Yarn "Sailboats." 1981 – 1984. Peel-and-Stick board, yarn pencil, different colored yarn, and instruction book. **$6.00.**

#749 Color With Yarn "Puppies At Play." 1981 – 1984. Same supplies as #748. **$6.00.**

#750 Color With Yarn "Bird and Flowers." 1981 – 1984. Same supplies as #748. **$6.00.**

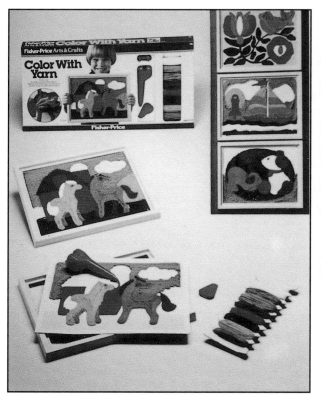

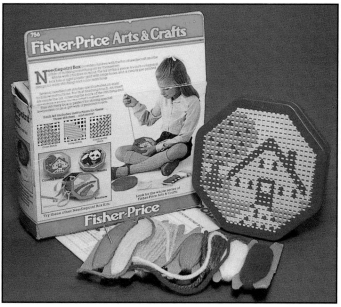

#756 Needlepoint Box "Country Home." Back of box. 1983 – 1984. Same supplies as #754. **$5.00.**

#751 Color With Yarn "Ponies." 1982 – 1984. Same supplies as #748. **$6.00.**

Not pictured
#754 Needlepoint Box "Panda." 1983 – 1984. Plastic octagonal box with lid. Lid has grid with printed design for color matching the six colors of yarn, dark blue, light blue, white, red, yellow, and green, metal needle, and insert for back of lid. **$5.00.**

#755 Needlepoint Box Rainbow. 1983 – 1984. Same supplies as #754. **$5.00.**

#756 "12 Days of Christmas" Pocket Radio. 1973 only. Wood case with plastic face and strap. **$25.00.**
Note: Back of a non-working radio can be rapped to free up the movement.

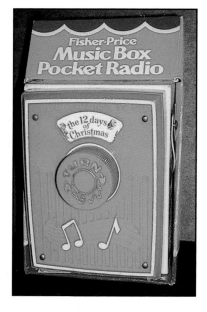

#757 Melody Push Chime. 1963 – 1966. Musical roller chime designed with storybook figures.

1967 – 1979 Musical roller chime designed with storybook figures. Polyethylene yoke, 17¾" long with round ball on end. **$10.00.**

1980 – 1988 Same as above with open grip handle instead of ball. **$5.00.**

1988 – 1992 Number changed (see #2018)

#758 "Mulberry Bush" Pocket Radio. 1970 – 1972. Wood case with plastic face. **$20.00.**

#758 Push-Along Clown. 1980 – 1981. Happy little clown's head bobs and spins. Makes a rattle sound when pushed, 16¾" handle with open grip. **$20.00.**

#759 "Do-Re-Mi" Pocket Radio. 1969 – 1973. Wood case with plastic face and strap. **$20.00.**

#760 Peek-A-Boo Block. 1970 – 1979. Squeeze bulb, flip-top lid opens, and figure pops up and disappears, making a squeak sound. **$15.00.**

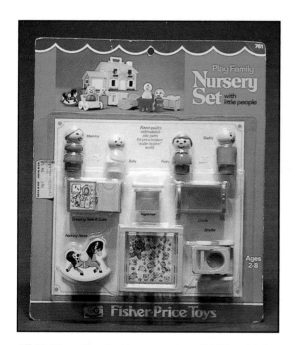

#761 Play Family Nursery Set. 1973 – 1984. Ten piece set. Playpen, cradle, high chair, stroller, rocking horse, dressing table, blue mom with blonde hair, green dad with heat stamped hair, blue girl with blonde hair, and baby with bib. Price is for set unopened. **$30.00.**

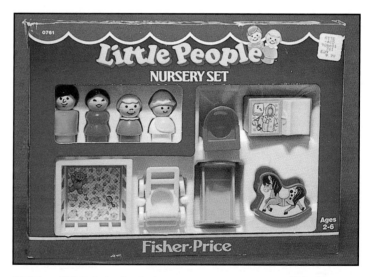

1985 – 1990 Baby had white bonnet. Loose set, **$10.00.**
Note: The descriptions of the figures are as pictured in 1973 catalogs and boxes. The figures and pieces could be in any color combination.

#762 "Raindrops" Pocket Radio. 1972 – 1977. Wood case with plastic face. **$25.00.**

#763 "I Whistle A Happy Tune" Pocket Radio. 1978 only. Wood case with plastic face and strap. **$20.00.**

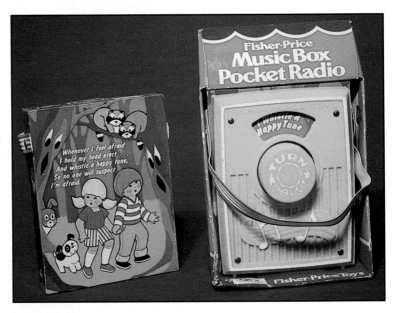

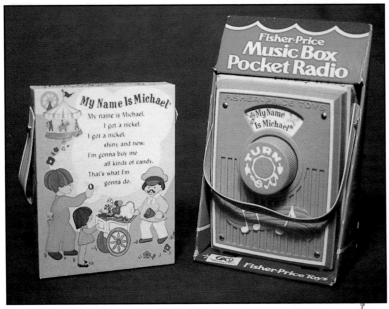

#764 "My Name Is Michael" Pocket Radio. 1975 – 1976. Wood case with plastic face and strap. **$15.00.**

#765 *Sesame Street Lacing Puppets "Big Bird and Ernie." 1984 only. Set of two precut and printed puppet halves with holes to lace up with laces.* **$10.00.**

#766 *"Where Has My Little Dog Gone" Pocket Radio. 1968 – 1970. Wood case with plastic face and strap.* **$25.00.**

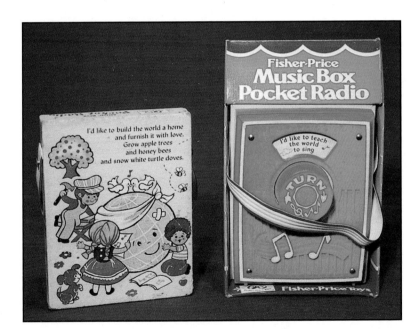

#766 *"I'd Like to Teach the World to Sing" Pocket Radio. 1977 – 1978. Wood case with plastic face and strap.* **$20.00.**

#766 *Sesame Street Lacing Puppets "Cookie Monster & Bert." 1984 only. Same description as #765.* **$6.00.**

#767 Sesame Street Lacing Puppets "Oscar & Grover." 1984 only. Same description as #765. **$6.00.**

#767 "Twinkle Twinkle Little Star" Pocket Radio. 1977 only. Wood case with plastic face and strap. **$25.00.**

Toy and photo courtesy of Ted Furcht.

#768 "Happy Birthday" Pocket Radio. 1971 – 1976. Wood case with plastic face. **$15.00.**

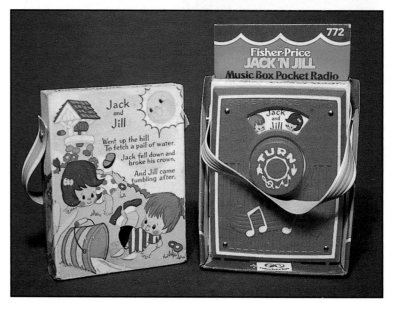

#772 "Jack & Jill" Pocket Radio. 1974 – 1976. Wood case with plastic face. **$20.00.**

#774 "Twinkle Twinkle Little Star" Pocket Radio. 1967 – 1971. Wood case with plastic face and strap. **$20.00.**

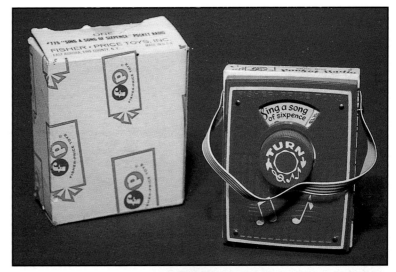

Toy and photo courtesy of Ted Furcht.

#775 "Sing a Song of Sixpence" Pocket Radio. 1967 – 1968. Wood case with plastic face and strap. **$25.00.**
Note: The box pictured with this radio is known as a shipper. This style of box was used when one ordered directly from Fisher-Price, or chain stores such as Sears.

#775 "Pop! Goes The Weasel" Pocket Radio. 1973 – 1975. Wood case with plastic face. **$20.00.**

Photo and toy courtesy of Ted Furcht.

#778 "Frère Jacques" Pocket Radio. 1967 – 1968. Wood case with plastic face. **$20.00.**

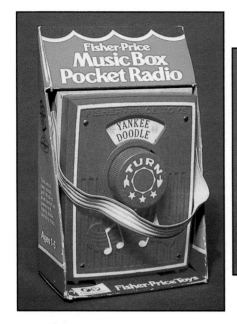

#779 "Yankee Doodle" Pocket Radio. 1976 only. Wood case with plastic face. **$20.00.**

#784 Picture Story Camera. 1967 – 1973. Color slide appears through viewer, eight pictures in all. Flash cube turns and click-clicks. Dial over see-through lens changes color to red, blue, yellow, or clear. **$10.00.**
Note: The boy molded on the right side of the plastic face is Eric Smith, son of John Smith, former art director. John did most of the art work on the Little People playset lithos. This image was also used in #112, #634, and #919.

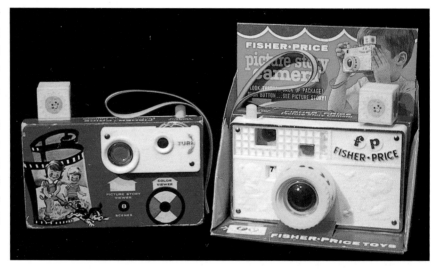

#786 Perky Penguin. 1973 – 1975. Squeeze bulb, beak opens and eyes look up and down, makes squawk-squawk sound. When pulled, feet flip-flop. **$25.00.**

#787 Creative Clay Tool Set. 1982 – 1983. Kit for shaping, stamping, and rolling clay. Eleven sculpting tools, ¾-pound of clay, and specially designed portable caddy. **$12.00.**

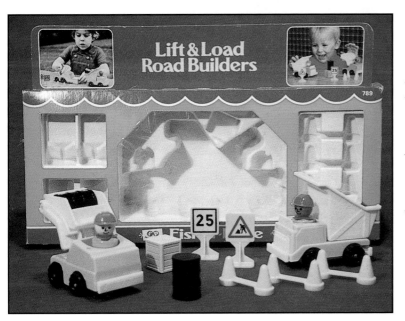

#789 Lift and Load Road Builders. 1978 – 1982. Twelve piece construction set. High lift and dump truck with spring action. Two barrels, one crate, three safety pylons, and two road signs, one 25 MPH outlined in black and one Men Working sign outlined in red. One black and one white construction worker with orange hard hats. **$20.00.**

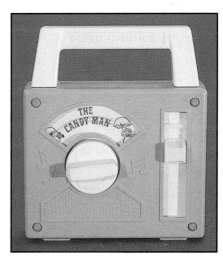

#790 "Candy Man" Tote-A-Tune Radio. 1979 – 1980. All plastic. **$10.00.**

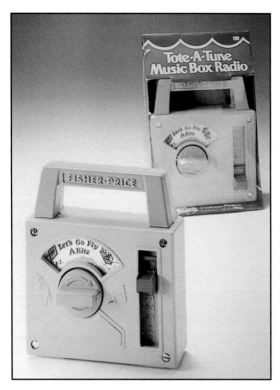

#791 "Let's Go Fly A Kite" Tote-A-Tune Radio. 1979 only. All plastic. **$10.00.**

#792 "Teddy Bears' Picnic" Music Box Radio. 1980 – 1981. All plastic. **$10.00.**

#793 "When You Wish Upon A Star" Tote-A-Tune Radio. 1981 – 1983. All plastic. **$10.00.**

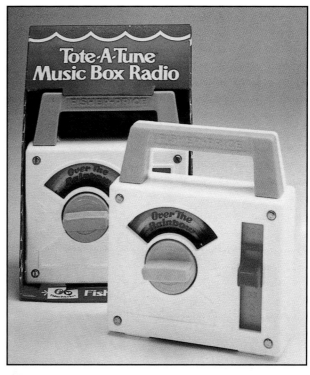

#794 *"Over The Rainbow" Tote-A-Tune Radio. 1982 – 1990. All white plastic with words "Over the Rainbow" on picture disk.* **$5.00.**

1991 *New picture disk litho with sun on it.* **$5.00.**

1992 *New number (see #5753)*

#795 *"Toyland" Tote-A-Tune Radio. 1984 – 1990. All green plastic with word "Toyland" in clouds.* **$5.00.**

1991 *Yellow case with a new picture disk litho with toy solders.* **$5.00.**

1992 *New number (see #5754)*

Toy courtesy of Gary Combs.

1979 — 1983 Puppets you can play mounted on a stick. Plastic figures 4" high with hole in their backs. White plastic puppet stick could be placed in the hole. All are jointed at the waist except Miss Piggy who is hollow and can double as a finger puppet.

#840 The Muppet Show Players Assortment.
#841 Kermit. **$5.00.**
#842 Fozzie. **$5.00.**

#843 Rowlf. **$5.00.**
#844 Miss Piggy. **$5.00.**

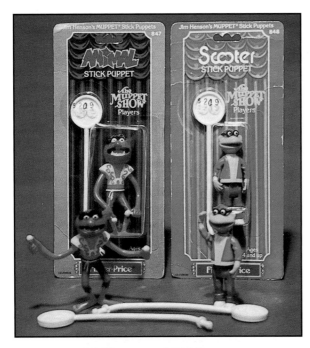

#847 Animal. **$10.00.**
#848 Scooter. **$10.00.**

#849 Gonzo. **$10.00.**

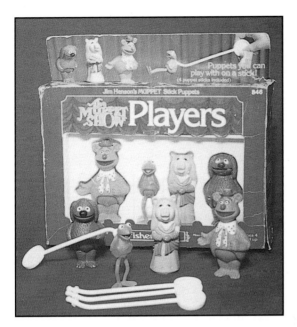

#846 The Muppet Show Players. 1979 – 1983. Set of stick puppets includes Kermit, Fozzie, Miss Piggy, and Rowlf. MIB. **$30.00.**

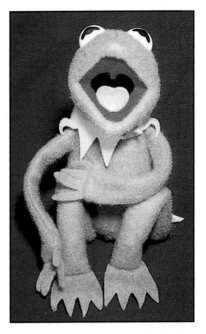

#850 Kermit the Frog. 1977 – 1983. A whimsical floppy-armed, floppy-legged plush toy. Velcro patches on arms and legs attach to his body. **$10.00.**

#851 Fozzie Bear. 1977 – 1978. A plump and cuddly plush toy with a silly grin and tweakable nose. Hat and tie are permanently attached. **$10.00.**

#852 Rowlf. 1977 – 1981. A shaggy plush Muppet puppet with big dog nose. His mouth moves and he has floppy ears and arms. **$10.00.**

#853 Scooter. 1978 – 1981. Plush body with green jacket, blue jeans, and sneakers. **$10.00.**

#854 Animal. 1978 – 1982. Hand puppet. Felt-covered plush with mouth that opens and closes. **$25.00.**

#855 Miss Piggy. 1979 – 1980. Plush Muppet puppet. Her mouth moves. **$10.00.**

#857 Kermit Dress-Up Puppet Doll. 1981 – 1984. Plush toy with removable raincoat, dickey with bow tie, and felt hat. **$10.00.**

#860 Kermit the Frog Hand Puppet. 1979 – 1983. A whimsical floppy-armed plush toy with movable mouth. **$10.00.**

#858 The Great Gonzo Dress-Up-Doll. 1982 – 1983. Plush toy with removable red cape, white undershirt, and silver gym shorts. **$15.00.**

#861 Fozzie Bear Hand Puppet. 1979 – 1982. Silly grin and tweakable nose. Hat and tie are permanently attached, movable mouth. **$10.00.**

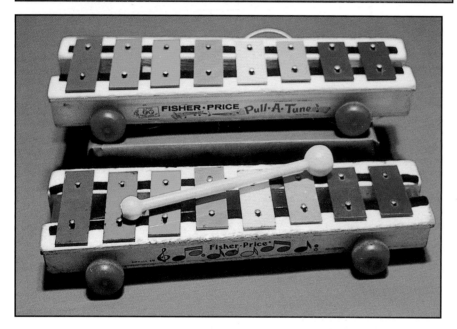

1966 – 1968. The wheels and mallet stayed the same but now there was a litho used on the sides. **$20.00.**

Note: 1957 – 1968. There are eight enameled keys colored red, orange, yellow, light green, dark green, light blue, dark blue and purple.

1969 – 1989 There are eight enameled keys but with new colors, red, dark orange, light orange, yellow, green, blue/green, dark blue, and purple.

1969 – 1977 The mallet and litho stayed the same but changed to plastic wheels. **$10.00.**

1978 only. New litho and the mallet was made of plastic. **$20.00.**

1979 – 1986 The only change made for this time period is the mallet was retooled to have a small ball on one end and a larger one on the other. It was also no longer attached to the end of the pull string. **$5.00.**

1987 – 1989 The base is all plastic. **$2.00.**

#870 Pull-A-Tune Xylophone. 1957 – 1965. This version had wooden base, wheels, and mallet. There is a ball on the end of the mallet, and the mallet is attached to the toy by a plastic pull string. There was no litho on it but the words "Fisher-Price Pull-A-Tune" are heat stamped on both sides. Four-page song book with color coded notes to the keys to teach children how to read musical notes. The songs in this book are Jingle Bells, Frère Jacques, This Old Man, and Twinkle Twinkle Little Star. The book is an English/French version. **$30.00.**

#887 Admiral of the Fleet. 1981 – 1982. Hat, coat, and pants. **$15.00.**

#888 Western Outfit. 1981 – 1982. Hat, scarf, vest, and chaps. **$12.00.**

#889 Kermit's Sleepwear Outfit. 1981 – 1982. Shirt, robe, and matching cap. **$12.00.**

#890 Miss Piggy Dress-Up Muppet Doll. 1981 – 1984. Plush toy with removable evening gown, turban, and gloves. **$12.00.**

#904 Beginner's Circus. 1965 – 1968. New beginner's version. Center ring, two ladders with connectors, dowel, ball, clown, bear, monkey, elephant, seal, giraffe, and instruction leaflet. **$60.00.**

#891 Miss Piggy's Sailor Outfit. 1981 – 1982. Sailor jump suit and cap. **$12.00.**

#892 Miss Piggy's Pigs in Space Outfit. 1981 – 1982. Blue shorts, silver jacket, blue gloves and boots. **$12.00.**

#893 Miss Piggy's Garden Party Outfit. 1981 – 1982. Full-length dress and hat. **$12.00.**

#894 Miss Piggy's Prima Ballerina Outfit. 1982 only. Dress with slippers. **$15.00.**

#909 Play Family Rooms 1972 – 1974. Sears only; lime green litho table with four chairs, red or blue TV, couch, two arm chairs, coffee table, and two single beds of the same color.

Note: Not all the living room and bedroom pieces are the same color. If six of the pieces are red, then the other five pieces are blue. Yellow sink, stove, and refrigerator with doors that open. White bathtub, toilet, litho scale, and sink. Yellow or turquoise wading pool with toy design, turquoise grill, yellow and turquoise flowered umbrella table with two captain chairs. Blue wood mom, blonde hair; green dad, heat stamped hair; blue girl, blonde hair; red boy, heat stamped hair; straight body dog; and cloth bag with string ties for the play pieces. **$200.00.** MIB. **$300.00 – $400.00.**

#910 Change-A-Tune Piano. 1969 – 1972. Strike keys to play one of three songs, "Pop Goes The Weasel," "This Old Man," and "The Muffin Man." **$30.00.**

Note: These are found more often not working than working. The reason is the foam under the keys that pushes the keys up to turn the cylinder is deteriorated. This problem can be fixed. Contact Ted Furcht after 7pm EST at (516)796-0790 for repair help.

Figures' names are Mr. and Mrs. Brown, Cathy, and Clem. Farm animal names are Horace Horse, Bossy Cow, Spot Dog, Pudgy Pig, Woolie Sheep, Rusty Rooster, and Henrietta Hen.

Courtesy of Cindy and Steve McMahon.

#915 Play Family Farm. 1968 – 1979. First version. Barn with masonite base. All wood blue dad and boy with yellow cowboy hat, yellow mom with white hair only, and green or blue girl with freckles, white collar and red or yellow hair with ponytails. Plastic animals with screws on their bellies: white horse with brown mane or black horse with white mane; white and brown cow; white lamb; black pig with white ears; brown dog; white and red hen; red and black rooster. Tractor and cart, one red and the other yellow; white trough; red silo with brown door and white lid and mouse on litho; four-piece white fence; and harness. **$30.00.**
1970 Horse could now be brown, white or black. The lamb could be all black with a white face. The black lamb is one of hardest of all the farm animals to find. Also the cow can be all black with white spots and in my opinion is the second hardest farm animal to find.
1974 The girl figures with ponytails were dropped from production, and by 1975 none of the sets had them.
1980 – 1984 Had a dark green plastic base and plastic figures. **$20.00.**
1985 Sears only. Had a brown plastic base, and pink pig from this point until the last year of production in 1990. **$20.00.**
1986 – 1990 Number and litho changed and base is a light green (see #2501).

Note: This is a hard set to pin down as to the colors of the animals. I have listed all the different colored animals in the back of this book under the miscellaneous section. It is safe to say that any of the animals with a screw on their bellies came with the masonite base set. Any of the animals without the screw are post 1975. It has been my experience that collectors want one each of the different styled barns and all of the different styled animals. In the 1971, 1974 & 1975 catalogs, Mom is a whoops. Her hair is sideways. The 1980 & 1981 catalogs have two girls pictured with this set in which is also a whoops. One has green body, white collar, freckles, and brown hair; second is blue body, white collar, and brown hair.

#916 Fisher-Price Zoo. 1984 – 1985. Twenty-nine piece play-set. The fixed hippo on the top of the building can be either purple, silver or brown. Three-piece vehicle train; orange or brown birdhouse/gazebo; tree; two parrots, yellow and orange with litho heads; blue or brown hippo and brown or blue goat, always opposite color of each other; elephant; seal; vulture; two monkeys, black and brown; ape; lion cub; four different shaped feeding trays; one round steak; one oval fruit; one square plant; one triangle hay; green picnic table with two benches; red mom with blonde or black hair; blue dad with heat stamped hair; yellow boy with red cap or orange boy with heat stamped hair; blue girl with blonde hair or yellow girl with brown hair; dark green zoo keeper with tan hat. **$25.00.**

1986 – 1987 The only differences are the dad is blue or green with molded brown or black hair, and the zoo keeper is light green with cap. Some or all of the lithos on the feeding trays could have an ID number.
Note: The picnic table and beaches could be blue, but is a very, very rare find. They have sold for as much as **$15.00.**

#919 Music Box Movie Camera. 1968 – 1970. Plays "This Old Man" when trigger is squeezed. Five picture disks with eight pictures on each disk: "Goldilocks and Three Bears," "Animals and Their Babies," "Visit to City," "Learning About Colors" and "Learning to Count." **$40.00.**
Note: The boy molded on the right side of the plastic face is Eric Smith, son of John Smith, former art director. John did most of the art work on the Little People playset lithos. This image was also used in #112, #634, and #784.

#923 Play Family School. 1971 – 1978. First version. Teacher with either yellow or green desk and chair, always opposite color of students' desks. Four figures with old-style school desks. Green boy with heat stamped hair, black boy with heat stamped hair, green girl with red hair, blue girl with blonde hair in ponytails. Teacher blue with blonde hair. Green and yellow swing with teeter-totter, green and yellow whirl-around, slide in either green or yellow, alphabet tray with letters A through Z, and seven extra letters in any combination, number tray with numbers 0 through 9, chalk and eraser. **$25.00.**

Note: The descriptions of the boy and girl figures are as pictured in 1971 catalogs and boxes. They could be in any color combination. Girl in photo is author's daughter, Christina, at age 5.

#928 Play Family Fire Station. 1980 – 1982. Seventeen piece playset. Turn crank on side of fire station, fire door opens, and bell rings. Chief's car, ambulance, fire truck with two hoses and stabilizer bars, practice tower, two-road barricades, two-piece ladder, three firemen, two with red hats and one with white hat, and Dalmatian dog. **$65.00.**

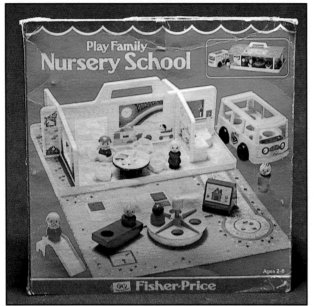

#929 Play Family Nursery School. 1978 – 1979. Twenty-two piece playset. Nursery room playset with removable cardboard roof/playground; round litho craft table with four captains chairs; blue easel, one side a house, the other a tree on a hill with flowers; kitchen sink; stove; bathroom sink, and commode, all white; blue teeter-totter; green and yellow merry-go-round; green or yellow slide; yellow mini school bus with green driver, heat stamped hair; blue teacher with blonde hair; and four preschoolers: green boy with heat stamped hair, black boy with heat stamped hair, red girl with blonde hair, and green girl with brown hair. **$50.00.**

Note: The descriptions of the boy and girl figures are as pictured in 1978 catalogs and boxes. They could be in any color combination.

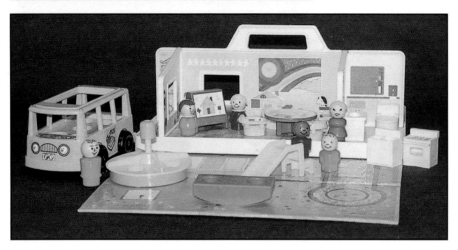

#930 Play Family Action Garage. 1970 – 1984. Ten piece playset. Masonite base and plastic two-level garage with elevator; gas pump; working grease rack; ramp and four cars, green, red, yellow and blue; four figures, three boys, yellow with red cap, red with heat stamped hair, green with heat stamped hair, and blue girl with blonde hair and ponytails; hand crank raises and lowers elevator, bell rings, and stop sign raises and lowers. In 1970 only, the pieces came inside a second box similar to the #952 Moving Van box. With second box. **$200.00.** Without second box. **$20.00.**

In **1971** Fisher-Price changed the inner box to this plain cardboard box with red print. They had changed the design of the box to help keep the outer box from crushing. **$20.00.**

1985 only. The rotating disk on top of the garage no longer has the heat stamped arrows and the stop sign's letter is raised and has no heat stamping. **$20.00.**

For the first year this set had a blue inner cardboard truck for the pieces. This truck ranges from **$50.00 – $200.00.**

1986 – 1990 New name and number changed (see #2504).
Note: The descriptions of the boy and girl figures are as pictured in 1970 catalogs and boxes. They could be in any color combination.

#931 Play Family Hospital. 1976 – 1978. Twenty-one piece playset. Hospital, ambulance with stretcher, X-ray machine, scale, operating table, wheel chair, two beds, two chairs, crib, bed screen, scrub sink, nurse with white mask, doctor and ambulance driver both have white bodies and one is black. Green dad with heat stamped hair, blue mom with blonde hair, red girl with blonde hair, and infant without bib. **$115.00.**
Note: This set came with only the pieces pictured in these colors. There were no exceptions.

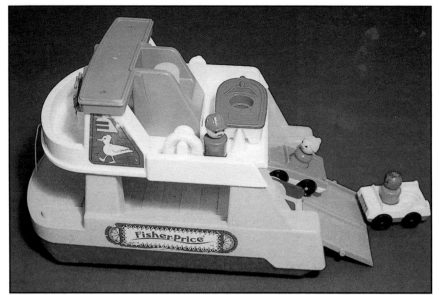

#932 Ferry Boat. 1979 – 1980. Eight piece playset. Boat floats and has wheels for floor play, double steering wheel and whistle on bridge, lower deck has a fold-down ramp and flip-up front and rear gates, one single and one two-passenger car, blue mom with blonde hair, orange dad, black, heat stamped hair, two yellow life preservers, and captain with dark blue body, mustache, and hat. **$45.00.**

Toy courtesy of Gary Combs.

#933 Play Family Jetport. 1981 – 1985. Twenty-two piece playset. Modern airport with blue plastic base. Has two boarding gates and crank on the roof that spins helicopter blades and radar antenna. Blue, yellow, and white twin engine jumbo jet with blue windshield. Jet makes motor sound when pushed, two pilots: short blue with blue cap, short blue with black body and blue cap, blue mom with blonde hair, tan dad with heat stamped hair, yellow boy with heat stamped hair, red girl with brown hair, light blue stewardess, one square brown and one blue round suitcase, helicopter with or without triangle stamping on blades, tractor with baggage car and fuel trailer, two-passenger car with luggage rack, four captain's chairs, and two small tables. **$30.00.**

1986 Name and number changed (see #2502).

Note: The descriptions of the boy and girl figures are as pictured in 1981 catalogs and boxes. They could be in any color combination.

#934 Play Family Western Town. 1982 – 1984. Nineteen piece playset. Western town. Green or tan buck-board wagon and stagecoach with removable roof. One black and one brown horse with circle on their bellies, hitching harnesses, removable saddle, crates, baggage, four-section fencing, red cowboy with black hat, yellow lady rancher with lime hat, blue sheriff with heat stamped star, and orange Indian. **$65.00.**

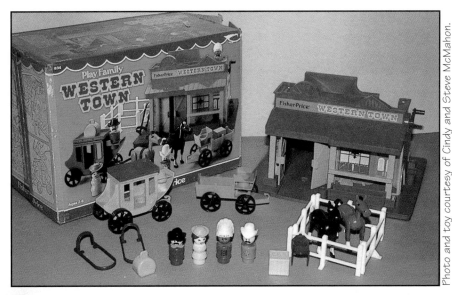

Photo and toy courtesy of Cindy and Steve McMahon.

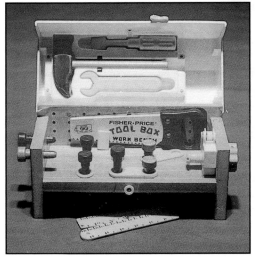

#935 Tool Box Work Bench. 1969 – 1971. Seventeen piece playset. Complete work bench in tool box with carrying handle. Hinged lid with storage compartment for claw hammer, wrench, and screwdriver. Bench holds saw, 18" ruler, four plastic nails, two nuts and bolts and connector cleats. Work surface has eight holes for pounding and fastening. **$25.00.**

#937 Play Family Sesame Street Clubhouse. 1977 – 1979. Fourteen piece playset. A magical playground with turn crank, Big Bird turns round and round in crow's nest. Trap door in roof sends figures out secret exit. Revolving door in back makes figures disappear and appear again. Attached tire swing, yellow slide, two-seater red wagon, yellow cable drum figures clip in, red and black jump rope swing, red, yellow, and blue, snap-together oil drums. Big Bird, Grover, Bert, Ernie, The Count, and Roosevelt Franklin. **$70.00.**
Note: If the tire swing is broken, it can be replaced.

#938 Play Family *Sesame Street* House. 1975 – 1976. Twenty-six piece playset. Sesame Street set with all the familiar loved characters from the TV series. Big Bird & nest, Oscar in trash can, Cookie Monster, Susan, Gordon, Mr. Hooper with heat stamped hair, Bert, Ernie, TV with Sesame Street litho, white five-rung ladder, two orange or brown beds, one-marked "B" and the other "E," table with pork chop litho, two chairs, sofa, coffee table, soda fountain & newsstand, fire hydrant, lamp post, mail box, garbage truck, chalk, and eraser. **$75.00.**

1977 – 1978 Oscar in trash can did not have a handle on the lid.

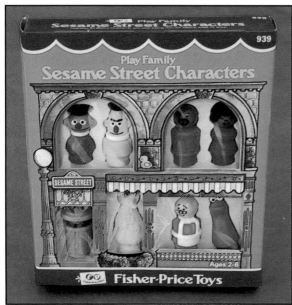

#939 *Sesame Street* Characters. 1976 – 1979 Bert, Ernie, Big Bird, Cookie Monster, Oscar, Susan, Gordon, and Mr. Hooper. **$4.00 – $8.00 each.** This set MIB has sold for as much as **$150.00.**

#940 Sesame Street Characters. 1977 – 1978. Sherlock Hemlock, Prairie Dawn, Herry Monster, and Snuffleupagus. **$10.00 – $20.00 each.**

Roosevelt Franklin, The Count, and Grover. **$5.00 – $10.00 each.**
This set MIB has sold for as much as **$475.00.**

#942 Play Family Lift & Load Depot. 1977 – 1979. Eighteen piece playset. Depot with crank-operated bucket. Roof top crane moves along track to shuttle cargo. Crank makes clicking motor sound. Dump truck, scoop loader, forklift, four pallets, two barrels, two gray and two tan crates, yellow sling for crane, one black and two white workers with orange hard hats and scarves. **$50.00.**

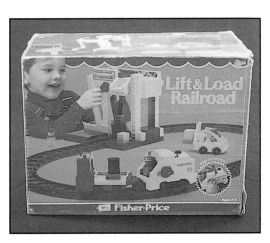

#943 Lift & Load Railroad. 1978 – 1979. Twenty-four piece playset. Locomotive with wind-up motor and detachable flat car. Seven-piece 93" oval track. Big depot with tunnel and freight dock with crank-operated crane. Green and yellow forklift, tan or brown crates, two barrels, four skids, orange sling, ramp, one black worker, and one white worker, both with orange hard hats, and tall light blue engineer with mustache. **$50.00.**

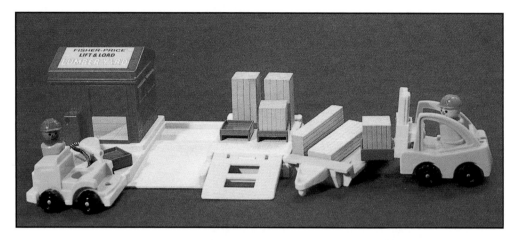

#944 Lift & Load Lumber Yard 1979 – 1981. Seventeen piece playset. Lumber yard with bay and loading dock with detachable yellow ramp. Two long, two short rectangular, and two square birch wood blocks with grooves cut in them. Green and yellow truck with flatbed trailer and spring action forklift, four stacking pallets, one black and one white worker, both with orange hard hats and scarves. **$50.00.**

#945 Offshore Cargo Base. 1979 – 1980. Twenty-two piece playset. Three interchangeable platforms. Helicopter deck, docking location and crane base, pivoting turret crane, one square and other rectangle floating pontoons, tug boat and barge, helicopter with 945 heat stamped on side, two sets of chains with hooks on each end, yellow net, two corn bags, two sets of pipes, two crates, dark blue captain with hat and mustache, one white and one black worker with green body, both with yellow hard hats and scarves, and one red diver with mask. **$65.00.**

Note: The diver looks more like a astronaut than a diver.

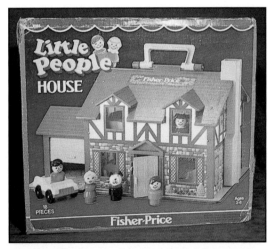

#952 Play Family House. 1969 only. First version: Masonite base two-story house with yellow roof, staircase with closet and litho. Yellow round kitchen table with four chairs, two twin and one double beds, two brown wing chairs and coffee table. Blue and white single passenger car with hook, wood blue mom with blonde hair, green dad with heat stamped hair, orange boy with heat stamped hair, blue girl with blonde hair and ponytails, and straight bodied dog with yellow collar. Play parts were packed in a cardboard delivery truck for this year only. **$535.00.**

1970 Same as above without cardboard delivery truck. **$35.00.**

1971 – 1979 Same as above with regular bodied dog and car without a hook. **$30.00.**

1980 – 1986 Same as above but new style litho, brown roof, and staircase were omitted. Furniture came in either yellow, white, orange, green, or brown. **$20.00.**
Note: The descriptions of the figures and pieces are as pictured in 1969 catalogs and boxes. The bed, kitchen, and living room sets could be in any color combination.

1987 – 1988 Same as #952, but house now has a green plastic base. The beds have a diamond pattern molded into the plastic in place of the foam. Dad and boy have molded hair. **$20.00.**

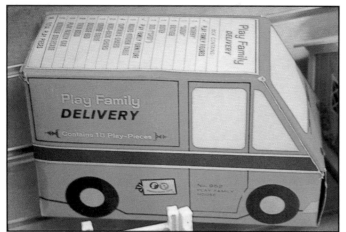

#952 Delivery Truck for yellow-roofed house. 1969 only. Cardboard moving truck has Fisher-Price Movers on the sides and a complete list of pieces on the roof and under side of van. We believe the play pieces came in the truck for this year only. This is, in my opinion, a starting price. **$500.00.**
Note: It has sold on the auction market for just over **$1,000.00.**

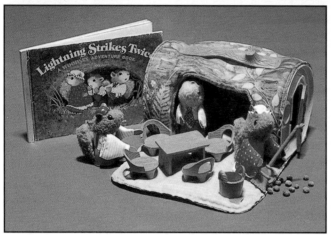

#960 Woodsey's Log House. 1979 – 1981. Log house made of foam, fabric, and vinyl, vinyl table with three chairs, bucket and broom, Woodsey's mom, dad, and boy, 32-page story book, "Lightning Strikes Twice." **$25.00.**

#961 Woodsey's Store. 1980 – 1981. Hollow tree. With vinyl potbellied stove, two chairs, push cart, cloth basket of fruit and vegetables, Grandma and Grandpa Woodsey; 32-page story book "Grandma and Grandpa's Opening." **$35.00.**

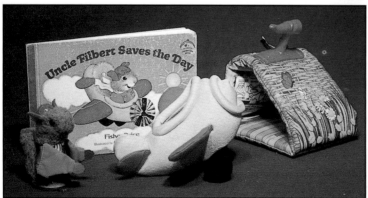

#962 Woodsey's Airport 1980 – 1981. Airplane and hanger made as **#960.** One Woodsey, Uncle Filbert; 32-page story book "Uncle Filbert Saves The Day." **$20.00.**

#969 Musical Ferris Wheel. 1966 – 1972. First version. When wound, ferris wheel revolves to "In The Good Old Summertime." Four all-wood straight body figures, red mom, green girl, blue boy with heat stamped hair and mad face, and dog with white ears. Seats have molded rod in middle to hold figures. **$50.00.**

1973 – 1980. Second version. Figures' bodies have shapes and came in wood, then wood and plastic, later on, all plastic. Green boy with red cowboy hat, blue girl, red hair with ponytails, red girl, blond hair, and dog with yellow collar. Seats no longer have rod on them. **$30.00.**
Note: The descriptions of the figures for both sets are as pictured in 1966 – 1973 catalogs and boxes. They could be in any color combination.

#978 Riding Horse. 1976 – 1978. Rolls along on wide wheels making clippity-clop sound, reins make "naaaa" sound when moved up and down. **$10.00.**

1979 – 1986 Reins no longer make "naaaa" sound. **$5.00.**
Note: This toy cleans up really nicely with a good washing and a little car wax.

#979 Dump Trucker Play Set. 1965 – 1967. Ten piece playset. Playset with three loading bays and three loading trucks, one each color and either square, circular or triangular dump bed; three wood balls; three figures, one smiling, one frowning, and another smiling or frowning with freckles and are all light or dark blue straight bodied. The trucks and loading bays had no set colors except that there were never two trucks or loading bays in the same color. **$75.00.**

1968 – 1970 The wood balls were changed to plastic. The reason this set can sell for more than the first version is the plastic balls were often smashed and lost. **$100.00.**

Note: The little girl used for this toy is Lori Inglis (see #125), and the boy is John Asthalter, son of Jack H. Asthalter, former marketing vice-president.

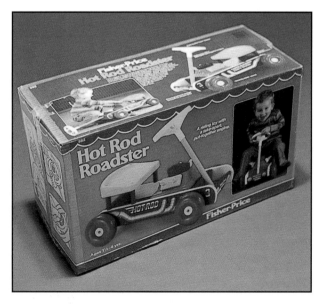

#982 Hot Rod Roadster. 1983 – 1984. Riding toy with clickety-click sound and four-piece take-apart engine. Push-button horn beep-beeps. **$45.00.**

#985 Play Family Houseboat. 1972 – 1976. Fifteen piece playset. Houseboat floats and makes putt-putt sound when pulled. Two yellow deck lounges, yellow grill, two yellow life preservers, table with lobster litho, two red chairs, blue and white speed boat, dad with white body and blue cap, blue mom with blonde hair, red girl with blonde hair, yellow boy with red cap, freckles, and dog. **$45.00.**

#987 Creative Coaster. 1964 – 1982. Riding toy with 18 blocks and six wood dowels. Beep-beep sounds, push button horn. Makes clickety-click engine sound. Steering wheel rotates and column swings forward so that coaster can become a pull toy. Some time in the mid-1970s, the dowels and seat were made of plastic. **$50.00.**

#987 Ride 'N Tote. 1964. This was a Sears exclusive that I have very little information on other than it is the same design as the #987 Creative Coaster and came with the same pieces. No value listed.

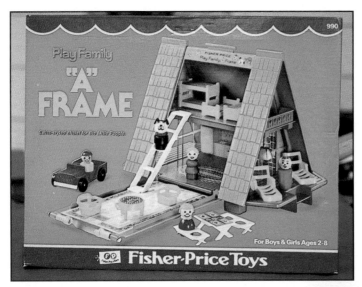

#990 Play Family "A" Frame. 1974 – 1976. White picnic table with steak litho and two benches, two yellow chairs, two yellow chaise lounges, yellow or red grill with three legs, three-rung ladder, four stackable bunk beds, blue mom with blonde hair, green dad with heat stamped hair, yellow boy with red cap, red girl with blonde hair, dog with red collar, and four-passenger Jeep. **$60.00.**

Note: The descriptions of the figures are as pictured in 1974 catalogs and boxes. They could be in any color combination. This is more likely to be the case with the boy and girl figures. Girl in photo is author's daughter, Christina, 7.

#991 Music Box Lacing Shoe, "Old Woman Who Lived in A Shoe." 1964 – 1967. Three red straight body figures, mom, boy with freckles, and girl. Round red and white shoe lace. **$60.00.**

#991 Play Family Circus Train. 1973 – 1978. Twelve piece playset. Engine with push button train whistle, gondola car, cage car, caboose, short ringmaster, red clown with yellow hat, short light blue engineer, elephant, bear, monkey, giraffe, and lion. The gondola car and cage car came in either green or blue. If the gondola car was green, the cage car would have been blue or vice versa. **$25.00.**

1979 – 1986 Gondola car and giraffe were omitted. **$15.00.**

1987 – 1990 New name and number (see #2581). **$10.00.**

#992 Play Family Car & Camper. 1980 – 1984. Fifteen piece playset. Red and white four-wheel drive station wagon with trailer camper that unfolds as pop-up tent. Set includes green picnic table with steak litho and two benches, two green lounge chairs, yellow grill, container that mounts onto camper, red trail bike, four-seater boat, blue mom, blonde hair; green dad, heat stamped hair; yellow boy, red cap; and red girl, blonde hair. **$35.00.**

1982 – 1984 The grill legs are a one-piece X shape. This is the first set to come with this new style grill.

Note: The descriptions of the figures are as pictured in 1980 – 1984 catalogs and boxes. The figures could be in any color combination.

#993 Play Family Castle. 1974 — 1977. Twenty-one piece play-set. Castle with flag mounted on spring. Yellow or red round table with steak litho and two short back chairs with crowns, two yellow or red thrones, dragon, one black and one brown horse, yellow or white harness for coach, yellow or white blan-keted saddle, coach, two yellow or red single and one double bed with crowns on headboard, wood and plastic King, Queen, Prince, Princess, woodsman, and plastic knight. **$100.00.**

1988 Classic collectors edition. This set is the same but without the flag and all plastic figures. **$125.00.**

#994 Play Family Camper. 1973 – 1976. Nineteen piece playset. Truck with motor sound and lift-off camper, rowboat, yellow trail bike, round red and yellow picnic table with spring-mounted umbrella, red picnic table with hot dog litho and four chairs, yellow or red grill with three legs, sink, toilet, red ladder, blue mom, blonde hair; green dad, heat stamped hair; yellow boy, red cap; red girl, blonde hair; and dog with yellow or blue collar. **$75.00.**

Note: The descriptions of the figures are as pictured in 1973 – 1974 catalogs and boxes. The red ladder is the hardest of all the Little People pieces to find. This set was sold both with and without the ladder. Without ladder **$65.00.**

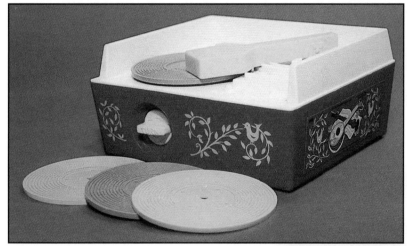

#995 Music Box Record Player 1971 – 1983. Red wind-up record player with five plastic records. **#1.** Jack and Jill / Humpty Dumpty **#2.** Twinkle, Twinkle Little Star/Au Clair de la Lune **#3.** London Bridge/ Oh Where Has My Little Dog Gone **#4.** Children's Marching Song/Camptown Races **#5.** Hickory Dickory Dock/Edelweiss. **$7.00.**

#995 Music Box Record Player Sesame Street. 1984 – 1987. Green wind-up record player with five plastic records. **#1, 2, 3 & 5** same as above. **#4.** One Of These Things/ "C" Is For Cookie. **$5.00.**

#996 Play Family Airport. 1972 – 1976. Nineteen piece playset. Blue airport with clear plastic round control tower and swing-out loading ramp, jetliner with turquoise color wings and wooden head pilot, action helicopter, revolving baggage's conveyor, tug tractor, two baggage carts, jet fueler, two passenger cars with luggage rack, four pieces luggage, two green round and two yellow square. Black wood and plastic pilot, short blue stewardess, blue mom with blonde hair, dark green dad with heat stamped hair, yellow boy with red cap, and blue girl with blonde hair and ponytails. Crank turns helicopter on post, spins rotor making whomp-whomp copter sound, and rotates baggage conveyor. **$65.00.**

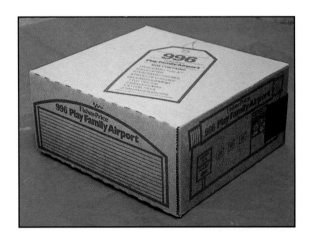

The plane and play pieces came packed in a brown cardboard box that fit inside the main box. Packing box only **$25.00.**
Note: The descriptions of the figures are as pictured in 1972 – 1976 catalogs and boxes. The boy and girl could be in any color combination.

#997 Musical Tick-Tock Clock. 1962 – 1963. Swiss music box plays "Grandfather's Clock" tune with tick-tock sound. Movable hands for teaching time. This version has a dark brown simulated wood grain litho with a light blue sky background. The sundial also had a light blue background. **$40.00.**

1964 – 1967 The only changes in this version are the litho was a much lighter brown and the light blue sky was removed. The sundial also was changed to a darker blue on the sun side of the dial and a very dark blue on the moon side. **$40.00.**

#997 Play Family Village. 1973 – 1977. Two-piece village with bridge to connect them, village has post office with mail box, firehouse with crank that sounds a realistic siren and overhead door that opens, dentist office, theater with seats, stage, and rooftop restaurant. Garage has crank-up car lift with ratchet sound, police station with jail and bunk, knob on roof opens cell door making a ratchet sound, barber shop, and apartment. Set includes 32 play pieces. Green and yellow table with umbrella, four yellow chairs, yellow grill, matching color sofa and coffee table, telephone booth with closing door, mail truck without hole in roof, and six coded letters fit matching door slots, gray mailman, police car, blue police girl with blonde hair and blue hat, fire engine, fireman with white hat, single bed, two-seater passenger car, sports car, black and white bodied dentist, dentist chair, white head and body barber, barber chair, blue mom with blonde hair, yellow boy with red cap, red girl with blonde hair, and dog with yellow or red collar. **$75.00.**

Note: The descriptions of the figures are as pictured in 1973 – 1977 catalogs and boxes. The boy and girl could be in any color combination.

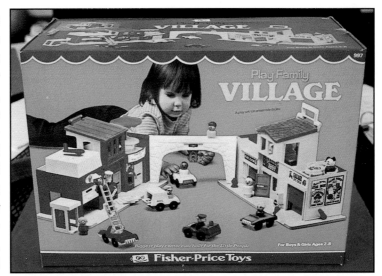

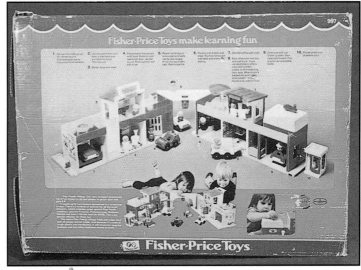

#998 Music Box Teaching Clock. 1968 – 1983. Little red schoolhouse litho. Plays "Grandfather's Clock" tune. Both clock's face and minute hand revolve. Adjustable hands for teaching time. **$40.00.**

#2017 Pull-Along Plane. 1981 – 1993. Sporty plane with putt-putt sound as propeller spins round. **$5.00.**
(See also #171)

#2018 Melody Push Chime. 1988 – 1992. Musical roller chime designed with storybook figures. Polyethylene yoke. **$2.00.**
(See also #757)

#2034 Little Snoopy. 1990 – 1993. Yip-yip sound when pulled, has a plastic shoe, spring-attached tail with plastic bead, and string attached at his lip. **$5.00.**

1991 Pull string is attached just below logo on his neck. **$3.00.**

1993 Snoopy is now made of all plastic. **$5.00.**

1994 Snoopy went to the plastic surgeon and got very fat and a Fisher-Price dog tag. S/A
(See also #693)

#2155 McDonald's Happy Meal. 1989 – 1990. Plastic Happy Meal Box with fries, hamburger, drink cup with lid, and special prize Funny Flute apple pie. **$15.00.**

#2204 Music Box TV. 1988 – 1991. All yellow plastic case with orange handle and knobs. Plays "London Bridge is Falling Down," and "Row, Row, Row Your Boat." **$4.00.**

#2205 Music Box Record Player. 1988 – 1992. Blue wind-up record player with five plastic records. #1. Jack and Jill / Humpty Dumpty #2. Twinkle, Twinkle Little Star/Au Clair de la Lune #3. London Bridge/ Oh Where Has My Little Dog Gone #4. Children's Marching Song/Camptown Races #5. Hickory Dickory Dock/Edelweiss. **$6.00.**
(See also #995)

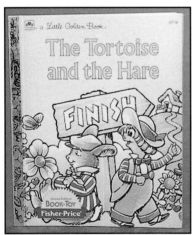

#2299 Fisher Price Classic Book and Toy. 1987 – 1988. (#2250 – #2253) A series of toys and books called "Classic Assortment." These were reissues of four well-known toys, each packed with special edition Little Golden Book with a story that relates to the toy. Each toy kept its original number along with the new Classics number. The Golden Book had a prominent logo, a gold sunburst with the words "Special Edition Book 'n Toy," a red ribbon with the Fisher-Price logo, and in the lower left-hand corner, the words "Fisher-Price." Add 30% with box.

#2250 Fire Engine. 1987 – 1988. **#720** Fire Engine with Little Golden Book "Fire Engine." MIB. **$40.00.**

#2251 Little Snoopy. 1987 – 1988. **#693** Little Snoopy with Little Golden Book "The Poky Little Puppy." MIB. **$40.00.**

#2252 Tag-Along Turtle. 1987 – 1988. **#644** Tag-Along Turtle with Little Golden Book "Tortoise and the Hare." MIB. **$40.00.**

#2253 Toot-Toot Engine. 1987 – 1988. **#643** Toot-Toot with Little Golden Book "Tootles." MIB. **$40.00.**

#2254 Tag-Along Turtle. 1992 – 1993. This is a reissue of the **#644**. The only change made are his feet are red. Turtle wags tail, rolls along on flipper-like feet, and makes ratchet sound. **$8.00.**
(See #644)

#2352 Little People Construction Set. 1985 only. Three orange and yellow construction trucks each with spring-loaded action. Front-end loader, dump truck, and bulldozer. One black and two white faced orange hard hat workers with blue bodies. Two road barricades, a road cone, two barrels, and crate. **$20.00.**

#2360 Jetliner. 1986 – 1988. Plastic plane with engine-like sound, white and yellow body with blue wings, and has "Fisher-Price" heat stamped on the rear. Hinged door and dark blue windshield. Four family figures with molded hair: yellow mom with brown hair, blue dad with brown hair, green boy with black hair, red girl with brown hair; one round dark or light blue and one square dark blue or brown luggage. Both pieces of luggage must be different colors. The figures to this set could have been any color with molded hair. **$10.00.**

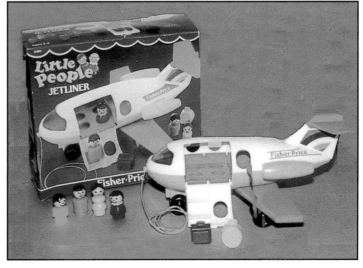

1989 Same as above but the words Fisher-Price are no longer on rear of plane. **$10.00.**
(See also #182)

Note: The descriptions of the figures for both sets are as pictured in 1986 – 1988 catalogs and boxes. The figures could be in any color combination.

#2361 Little People Fire Truck. 1989 – 1990. Fire truck with rotating light and ringing bell. Two section extension ladder, hydrant, yellow hoses, two firemen with white hats and hands, and Dalmatian dog. **$10.00.**

#2391. Jetliner. 1990 only with this number. This jet is the same as the **#2360** with the words "Fisher-Price" no longer on rear of plane. Four figures in any color with molded hair, and one round dark or light blue and one square dark blue or brown suitcase. **$8.00.**

#2448 Little People Vehicles Farm Fun. 1985 – 1990. Tractor with cart, red rooster, one feed bag, one blue farmer with yellow cowboy hat, and dog. **$7.00.**
Price for feed bag alone. **$3.00.**
(See also #636)

#2449 Little People Vehicles Air Lift Copter. 1985 – 1990. Copter with rescue cage, crate, and green pilot with cap. **$5.00.**

#2450 Little People Vehicles Race Car. 1985 – 1990. Race car, black driver with helmet. **$2.00.**
(See also #347)

#2451 Little People Vehicles Motorcycle. 1985 – 1990. Yellow motorcycle and blue figure with white helmet. **$6.00.**

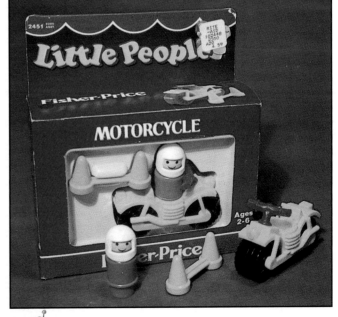

#2453 Beauty Salon. 1990 only. Interlocks with sets **#2454** and **#2455** to make a mini town. Came with a single passenger pink car and blue girl with blonde hair only. **$20.00.**

#2454 Drive-in Movie. 1990 only. Interlocks with sets **#2453** and **#2455** to make a mini town. Pictures pass by screen when knob is turned. Came with a yellow single passenger car and blue boy with black molded hair only. **$20.00.**

#2455 Gas Station. 1990 only. Interlocks with sets **#2453** and **#2454** to make a mini town. Came with a red single passenger car and yellow boy with brown molded hair only. **$20.00.**

#2500 Little People Main Street. 1986 – 1990. Twenty-four piece town. Fire truck and fireman with white hat and hands, two ramps, taxi, mail truck with a horn and words "Post Mail" on side, blue driver with blue cap, seven-coded letters match doors, mail box, traffic light, fire hydrant, yellow parking meter, yellow pay phone, red stop sign, red mom with blonde hair, lime girl with yellow hair, and green grocery store clerk with white apron and hair. **$50.00.**

1989 New style mail truck had a hole in roof and "Mail" stamped on the side. **$50.00.**

1990 The pay phone, parking meter, taxi, and storekeeper were omitted. **$40.00.**
Note: As best I know, the figures and pieces were never different than the ones listed. The pay phone, stop sign, and parking meter could be blue but are very, very rare finds. These three blue pieces have sold for as much as **$15.00 each.**

#2501 Little People Farm. 1986 – 1989. Farm with green plastic base and red loft doors. Blue dad and red boy with cowboy hats, green girl with blonde hair, yellow bodied mom with white hair, horse, cow, lamb, pink pig, dog, hen and rooster, animals do not have screws on their bellies. Tractor, cart, trough, four-piece fence, and silo with sunflowers on litho and ribs on lid. **$20.00.**

1990 only. The barn roof is imprinted with horseshoes. The girl, dog, water trough, and harness were omitted. **$20.00.**
Note: The descriptions of the figures are as pictured in 1986 – 1990 catalogs and boxes. The dad, boy, and girl could be in any color combination. (See also #915)

Photo and toy courtesy of Cindy and Steve McMahon.

#2502 Little People Airport. 1986 – 1989. Twenty-two piece playset airport. This is the same as the **#933** set but the base was changed to green and the jet to yellow, orange, and white. Has two boarding gates and crank on the roof that spins helicopter blades, and radar antenna. One white tall and one black short pilot, light blue stewardess, blue mom with yellow hair, green dad and yellow boy with brown or black molded hair, girl with brown hair, one round dark or light blue and one square dark blue or brown luggage. Both pieces of luggage must be different colors, helicopter with or without triangle stamping on blades, tractor with baggage car and fuel trailer. Four brown captain's chairs and two orange tables. **$15.00.**

1990 only. The base did not have the radar antenna and pull-down barrier arm. The stewardess, one pilot, one table, and two chairs were omitted. **$15.00.**
Note: The radar dish is either brown, the rarest, or red, the most common. The descriptions of the figures are as pictured in 1986 catalogs and boxes. The Play Family figures could be in any color combination.
(See also #933)

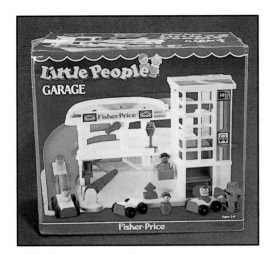

#2504 Little People Garage. 1986 only. Plastic two-level garage with crank lift elevator, red ramp and masonite base with bright blue color, green grease rack and four cars, green, red, yellow and blue. Elevator bell rings and stop sign raises and lowers. Red girl with brown molded hair, black boy, orange boy with molded hair and yellow boy with baseball cap. Bodies may be of other colors. Very rare. **$55.00.**

1987 – 1989 A few changes were made. The base was made of yellow plastic with a blue ramp. Figures are now girl with molded hair, black boy with black molded hair, and white boy with baseball cap. Three one-seater cars in red, blue, green, or yellow. Green parking meter, fire hydrant, green pay phone, green movable gas pump, and grease rack. **$20.00.**

1990 The parking meter, pay phone, fire hydrant, one car, and one figure were omitted. **$13.00.**
Note: The descriptions of the figures and pieces are as pictured in 1986 – 1990 catalogs and boxes. The figures and pieces could be in any color combination. (See also #930.) The girl in the photo is the author's daughter, Christina, age 7.

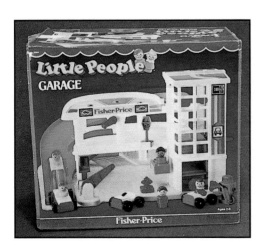

#2524 The Little People Cruise Boat. 1989 – 1990. Four-piece playset great for tub or pool play. S.S. Tadpole with built-in pool and diving board, gang plank for boarding, observation deck, and fishing pole with fish. Fishing chair flips up revealing cabin with two beds. Steering wheel has ratcheting sound. Also came with white life preserver, white bearded captain and boy with green body and yellow hair. This style boy figure came with this set only. **$20.00.**

#2525 Little People Playground Accessory Set for #95. 1986 – 1990. Green base with airplane and rocking horse attached to springs, slide, yellow and orange swing set and merry-go-round, blue climbing cube, orange boy with brown hair, and green girl with blonde hair. **$15.00.**
Note: The descriptions of the figures are as pictured in 1986 – 1990 catalogs and boxes. The figures could be in any color combination.

#2526 Little People Pool Accessory set for #952. 1986 – 1989. Off-white base with built-in pool. Slide in either yellow or orange, lifeguard chair and diving board in either yellow or green, umbrella table in either green and yellow or orange and yellow, two lounge chairs, one orange and one yellow, black barbecue grill, yellow life preserver, boy and girl figures with molded hair and any color body. **$15.00.**
Note: The descriptions of the figures are as pictured in 1986 – 1990 catalogs and boxes. The figures could be in any color combination.

#2550 Little People School. 1988 – 1989. Thirteen piece playset. School has a pull-out playground with attached teeter-totter, slide, and balance beam. School has a clock, alphabet scroll, and chalk board. Includes orange, red, and blue jump rope, white play barrel, stop sign, white flag with F-P, two figures on litho, yellow skateboard, yellow school bus, box of chalk, red teacher with yellow hair, black girl with black hair and green body, white girl with brown hair and orange body, yellow boy with baseball hat, and blue boy with black hair. **$30.00.**

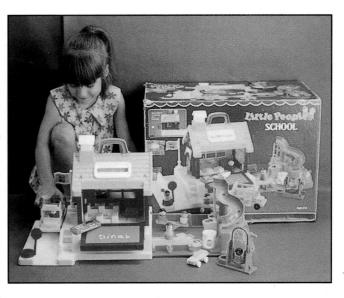

1990 There are three notable changes that were made to this playset. This is the only set pictured in any of the catalogs with the new style boy and girl figures pictured in them. The alphabet scroll was no longer one of the features. The roof has litho instead. Three of the figures have new facial features: the school teacher has half circle glasses, the orange figured girl has round glasses, and the blue boy has an Oriental look. The black girl with green body and boy with baseball hat did not change. The skateboard was also omitted. **$45.00.**

Note: The descriptions of the figures are as pictured in 1988 – 1990 catalogs and boxes. The figures could be a different color, only if Fisher-Price ran out of one set.

#2551 Little People Neighborhood. 1989 – 1989. Deluxe playset is really two different homes that connect with a brown treehouse with yellow door. Also features an automatic garage door opener, basketball set with tethered ball, swimming pool, upper deck with chute, pop-up trash can, and hinged skylight. Yellow or yellow and white passenger car with front and back seat, one blue or yellow over stuffed chair, two blue single beds with teddy bear quilt, one yellow or white double bed with imprinted quilt pattern, yellow ladder for the treehouse, light blue one-piece bath set, yellow one-piece kitchen set, yellow or brown round table with two chairs. Colors do not need to match. Red mom, blonde hair; blue dad, brown hair; yellow boy, brown hair; red girl, blonde hair, and dog. **$45.00.**

1990 Mom has glasses. **$50.00.**

Note: The descriptions of the figures are as pictured in 1986 – 1990 catalogs and boxes. The figures could be in a different color, only if Fisher-Price ran out of one set.

#2552 McDonald's Restaurant. 1990. First version. Features include a pull-out playground with slide, shake shaker, gobbling burger slide, and merry-go-round. Automatic opening front door, drive-thru window with slide-out tray, order counter, cooking area, and table. Blue or yellow and white car with front and back seat, brown trash can, golden arches, fry coaster, red mom, blonde hair; yellow boy, black hair; red girl, brown hair. Figures may be any color hair and body. Ronald and Hamburglar. **$70.00.**

1991-1992 The second version had the same pieces with the bigger Little People. **$50.00.**

#2580 Little People Little Mart. 1987 – 1989. Convenience store service station with car wash. Automatic door, clicking gas pump, and cashier counter. Yellow pay phone, orange shopping cart with bag of groceries, all blue or green car with front and back seat, red mom, blonde hair; green dad, black hair; police girl, dog, and orange tow truck. **$20.00.**
Note: The pay phone could be blue but is a very, very rare find. It has sold for as much as. **$15.00.** The figures are as listed in the 1987 – 1989 catalogs and boxes. The mom and dad figures could be in any color combination.

#2581 Little People Express Train. 1987 – 1990. Eleven piece train set. Engine with toot-toot sound, flat car, and caboose with doors that open. Two cars, one single seat and one with front and back seat in all yellow or all red, square and round suitcase in blue, dark blue or yellow, engineer with mustache, blue mom, blonde hair; green dad, black hair; and dog. **$15.00.**

1990 Both cars and dog were omitted (see also #991).
Note: The figures are as listed in the 1987 – 1990 catalogs and boxes. The mom and dad figures could be in any color combination.

#2582 Little People Floating Marina. 1988 – 1990. Nine piece playset for the tub or pool. Marina, orange or yellow row boat, red and white captain's boat, sea plane, yellow life jacket, removable rotating light beacon, three figures: captain with beard, green girl with blonde hair, and orange boy with brown hair. **$15.00.**

1989 & 1990 The sea plane was omitted.
Note: The figures are as listed in the 1987 – 1990 catalogs and boxes. The boy and girl figures could be in any color combination.

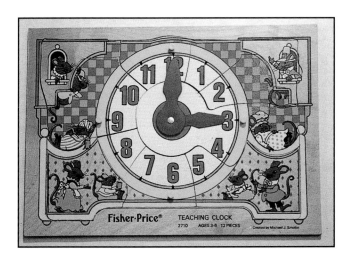

#2710 Teaching Clock, Pick-Up & Peek wood puzzle. 1985 – 1988. Twelve pieces. Clock with moving hands. **$15.00.**

#2711 Barn, Pick-Up & Peek wood puzzle. 1985 – 1988. Ten pieces. Red barn with various farm animals. **$15.00.**

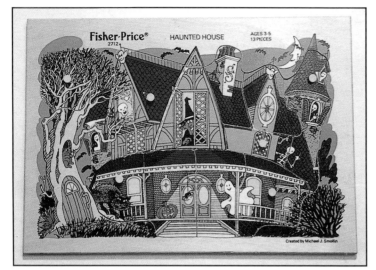

#2712 Haunted House, Pick-Up & Peek wood puzzle. 1985 – 1988. Thirteen pieces. Old house with various spooky figures. **$15.00.**

#2713 Dogs and Puppies, Pick-Up & Peek wood puzzle. 1985 – 1988. Ten pieces. Dog with leash and four puppies. **$15.00.**

#2714 Bears and Cubs, Pick-Up & Peek wood puzzle. 1985 – 1988. Ten pieces. Mother bear in rocker and three cubs playing. **$15.00.**

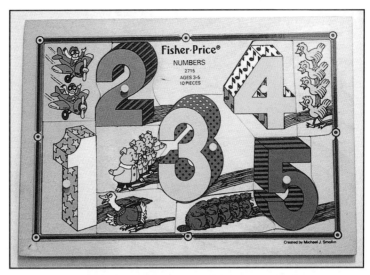

#2715 Numbers, Pick-Up & Peek wood puzzle. 1985 – 1988. Ten pieces. Numbers 1 – 5, in 3-D design. **$15.00.**

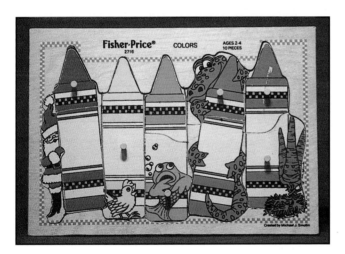

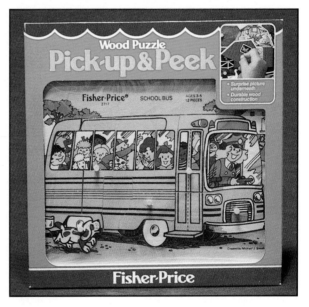

#2716 Colors, Pick-Up & Peek wood puzzle. 1985 – 1988. Ten pieces. Five colored crayons red, yellow, blue, green, and orange. **$15.00.**

#2717 School Bus, Pick-Up & Peek wood puzzle. 1985 – 1988. Twelve pieces. School bus full of kids and driver. **$15.00.**

#2720 Little Bo Peep, Pick-Up & Peek wood puzzle. 1985 – 1988. Six pieces. Little Bo Peep looking for her sheep. **$15.00.**

#2721 Hats, Pick-Up & Peek wood puzzle. 1985 – 1988. Six pieces. Fireman's hat, nurse, policeman, Santa Claus, and cowboy hats. **$15.00.**

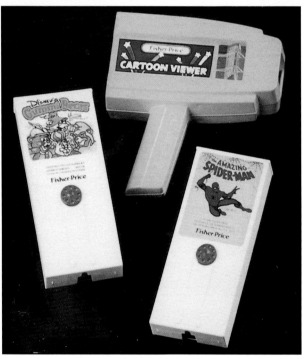

#3011 Spiderman Cartridge and Viewer. 1986 – 1987. A new design viewer with cartridge; viewer plastic is brighter yellow, and litho is blue with streaking stars. **$10.00.**

#3012 Gummi Bears Cartridge and Viewer. Same description as #3011. **$10.00.**

Not pictured
#3018 Viewer Cartridge. 1986 – 1987. "Who is Spider-man?," white cartridge. **$8.00.**

#3022 Viewer Cartridge. 1986 – 1987. "Gummies to the Rescue." **$8.00.**

#3016 Viewer Cartridge. 1986 – 1987. "Calvin Rides The Quick Tunnel," white cartridge. **$8.00.**

#3017 Viewer Cartridge. 1986 – 1987. "The Water Wheel Adventure," white cartridge. **$8.00.**

#3021 Viewer Cartridge. 1986 – 1987. Spider-man and his Amazing Friends in "Sunfire." **$8.00.**

#3019 Viewer Cartridge. 1986 – 1987. "The Incredible Shrinking Spider-man," white cartridge. **$8.00.**

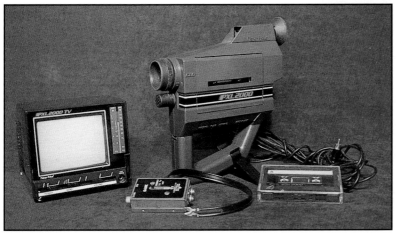

#3300 PXL 2000 Camcorder. 1988 – 1989. Records both audio and video on high bias audio cassettes. Set includes the PXL 2000 Camcorder, mini tripod stand, TV hook-up accessories, one C-90 high bias cassette tape, six AA batteries and instruction booklet. **$325.00.**

Not pictured

#3305 PXL 2000 Deluxe Camcorder System. 1988 – 1989. Same as #3300 but with a 4½" black and white monitor that operates as TV. **$350.00.**

#3320 PXL 2000 Camcorder Case. 1988 – 1989. Soft shell gray and blue nylon case with pockets for tapes and wires. **$20.00.**

#3325 PXL 2000 Tape Twin Pack. 1988 – 1989. Two blank C-90 cassettes with recording time of five minutes each side. **$12.00.**

#3321 PXL 2000 Action Strap. 1988 – 1989. Strap with clip-on harness, storage for extra batteries, and cassette. Can be used as shoulder strap or belt for on-the-go recording fun. **$15.00.**

#4009 Special Birthday Mandy. 1985 only. Mandy dressed in a pink party dress, lace stockings, and party hat. Also came with a surprise gift for child. **$50.00.**

Not pictured
#4108 Springtime Party Dress Outfit & Pattern. 1985 only. Turquoise dress, straw hat, and shoes. **$10.00.**

#4109 Cheerleader Outfit and Pattern. 1985 only. Knit sweater, skirt, socks, sneakers, headband, and two pom-pons. **$10.00.**

#4110 Aerobics Outfit and Pattern. 1985 only. Magenta and turquoise sweatshirt, mini skirt, headband, tights, leg warmers, sneakers, and gold purse. **$10.00.**

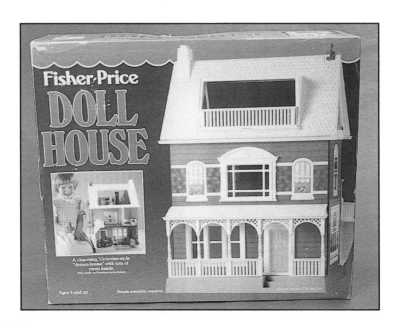

#4300 Fisher-Price Doll House. 1985 only. This is very similar to the #250 doll house. This house is pink with a roofed porch with railings. Came with four family figures, set #265, spiral staircase, decorating assembly guide, and two straps to hold house together. **$50.00.**

#4325 Desk & Clock. 1985 only. Roll-top desk with swivel chair and grandfather clock with movable hands and design on wood front. The desk is the same as #261. Clock is close to #262. **$8.00.**

#4326 Piano & Rocker. 1985 only. White and pink grand piano with stool and pink bent wood style rocker. **$15.00.**
(See also #262 & 285)

#4327 Kitchen Set. 1985 only. Double door refrigerator, oven with microwave and sink with three drawers. **$12.00.**

#4328 Bathroom Set. 1985 only. Brass claw leg tub, white and light blue combination sink and toilet unit. **$12.00.**
(See also #253)

#4329 Living Room Set. 1985 only. Pink sofa with two pillows and oval coffee table. **$6.00.**
Also pictured are the **#0255**, **#0260**, **#0264**, **#0257**, and **#0268** of 1985.

#4330 Deluxe Hutch Set With Lights. 1985 only. Pink Victorian hutch with compartment for AA batteries, pink table lamp with Tiffany-style shades and floor lamp with brass stem and clear shade. **$15.00.**
(See also #263)

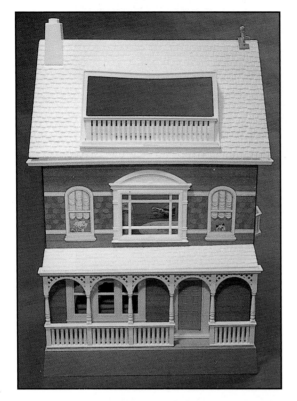

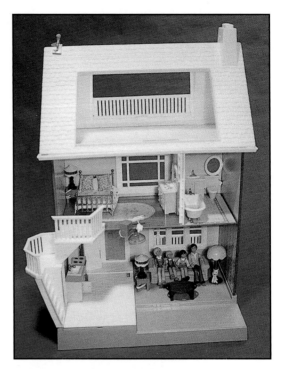

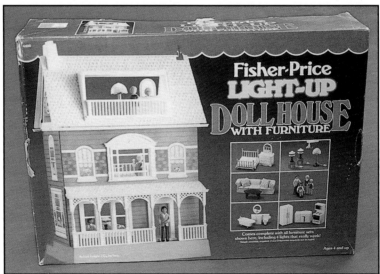

#4400. 1985 only. This is the same style and color as the #4300 doll house but with lighted features. Came with four lights, one ceiling, one brass floor lamp, two table lamps, four family figures set #265, living room set #4329, kitchen set #4327, bathroom set #4328, bedroom set #255, spiral staircase, decorating/assembly guide, and two straps to hold house together. **$75.00.**

#4500 Husky Helper Assortment. 1985 – 1986. Six different workmen with separate accessories. Policeman with walkie-talkie and clipboard; mechanic with wrench and drill; astronaut with two-piece jet pack; firefighter with fire extinguisher backpack; race car driver with gas tank; construction worker with shovel and sign. Set **$4.00.**
MOC. **$15.00.**

Not pictured
#4508 Hook and Ladder. 1985 only. Renumbered. See #319 for picture and description. **$20.00.**

#4512 Police Patrol Squad. 1985 – 1986. Renumbered. See #332 for picture and description. **$20.00.**

#4516 Rodeo Rig. 1985 only. Renumbered. See #330 for picture and description. **$20.00.**

#4520 Highway Dump Truck. 1985 – 1986 (similar to #328). Truck has working tailgate and handle for dumping load, removable cab roof for access to driver's seat, and figure. **$20.00.**

#4521 Dozer Loader. 1985 – 1986 (similar to #329). Dual shift levers to raise bucket and dump load, and figure. **$15.00.**

#4523 Gravel Hauler. 1985 – 1986 (similar to #327). Trailer yellow and gold, cab was black. **$15.00.**

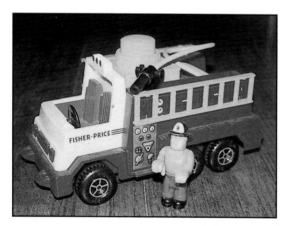

#4524 Fire Pumper. 1985 – 1986 (similar to #336). Enclosed cab with removable roof, two white ladders, water hose, and hand-operated water pump. Husky firefighter figure. **$15.00.**

#4550 Chevy S-10 4x4. 1985 only. Realistically styled Chevy S-10 Maxi Cab 4x4 with a fold-down tailgate, super-grip tires and sunroof. Removable roll/light bar doubles as a working winch when put on front or rear of truck. Off-road Husky figure. **$25.00.**

#4551 Pontiac Firebird. 1985 only. T-top roof, slick racing tires, and flip-up headlights. Husky Street Racer figure. **$25.00.**

#4552 Jeep CJ-7 Renegade. 1985 only. Has an open-style roof, fold-down windshield, super grip tires, four-wheel working suspension, roll/light bar, and removable spare tire. Husky Explorer figure. **$25.00.**

#4580 Power Tow. 1985 – 1986 (similar to #338). Wind-up motor that runs for 40 feet and makes engine sounds as it goes. Husky figured included. **$20.00.**

#4581 Power Dump Truck. 1985 – 1986. Dump truck with dual shift levers for dumping action, engine sounds. Truck is yellow and gold color with Husky figure. **$20.00.**

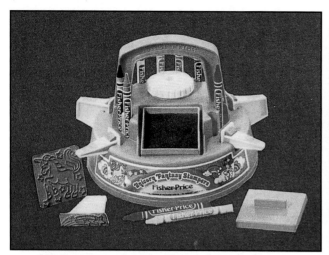

#5526 Stamping Assortments Unicorn Fantasy Stamper. 1985 – 1986. Pink plastic caddy, six stamps with handles, 10 crayons and sharpener, decal sheet, inked-pad with lid, and idea book. **$15.00.** (Same as 1984 #745)

#5771 Starting Stitchery Assortments "Heart." 1985 – 1986. Plastic grid with holes and printed design, six colors of yarn, green, red, orange, light blue, yellow, and dark blue, two plastic needles, snap-in frame, and instructions. **$8.00.**

#5772 Starting Stitchery Assortments "Ice Cream Cone." 1985 – 1986 (same as #5771 & #741). **$8.00.**
Note: Girl in photo is author's daughter, Dinah, age 8.

Not pictured
#5754 "Toyland" Music Box Radio. 1992 – 1993. Blue, red, and yellow plastic case with green knob. **$5.00.**
#5791 Needlepoint Box Assortments "Ballerina." 1985 – 1986. Plastic octagonal box with lid. Lid has grid with printed design for color matching the six colors of yarn, dark blue, light blue, white, red, yellow, and green, metal needle, and insert for back of lid. **$8.00.**

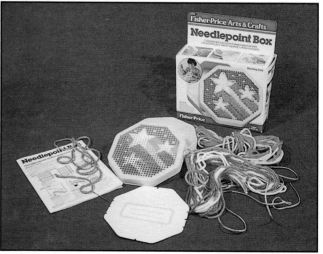

#5792 Needlepoint Box Assortments "Shooting Star." 1985 – 1986. Plastic octagonal box with lid (same as #5791 & #754). **$8.00.**

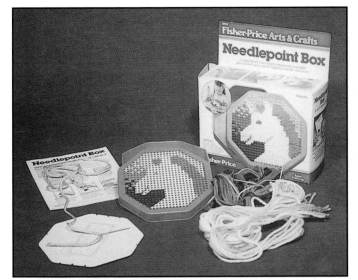

#5793 Needlepoint Box Assortments "Unicorn." 1985 – 1986. Plastic octagonal box with lid (same as #5791 & #754). **$8.00.**

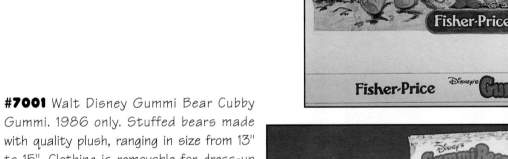

#7001 Walt Disney Gummi Bear Cubby Gummi. 1986 only. Stuffed bears made with quality plush, ranging in size from 13" to 15". Clothing is removable for dress-up fun. Character's biography and legend on each box. **$10.00.**

#7002 Walt Disney Gummi Bear Zummi Gummi. 1986. **$10.00.**

#7003 Walt Disney Gummi Bear Tummi Gummi. 1986 only. **$10.00.**

#7004 Walt Disney Gummi Bear Sunni Gummi. 1986 only. **$10.00.**

#7005 Walt Disney Gummi Bear Guffi Gummi. 1986 only. **$10.00.**

#7016 Walt Disney Gummi Bear Bouncer Cubbi Gummi. 1986 only. Plush bear bounces and has a rubber ball inside. **$6.00.**

#7006 Walt Disney Gummi Bear Grammi Gummi. 1986 only. Same as #7001. **$10.00.**

#7017 Walt Disney Gummi Bear Bouncer Zummi Gummi. 1986 only. **$6.00.**

#7019 Walt Disney Gummi Bear Bouncer Sunni Gummi. 1986 only. **$6.00.**

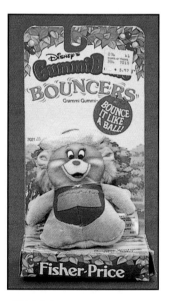

#7018 Walt Disney Gummi Bear Bouncer Tummi Gummi. 1986 only. **$6.00.**

#7020 Walt Disney Gummi Bear Bouncer Gruffi Gummi. 1986 only. **$6.00.**

#7021 Walt Disney Gummi Bear Bouncer Grammi Gummi. 1986 only. **$6.00.**

#7031 Walt Disney Gummi Bear Poseable Figures Cubby Gummi. 1986 only. Vinyl figures jointed at the head, arms, and legs. **$7.00.**

#7033 Walt Disney Gummi Bear Poseable Figures Tummi Gummi. 1986 only. **$7.00.**

#7034 Walt Disney Gummi Bear Poseable Figures Sunni Gummi. 1986 only. **$7.00.**

#7032 Walt Disney Gummi Bear Poseable Figures Zummi Gummi. 1986 only. **$7.00.**

#7035 Walt Disney Gummi Bear Poseable Figures Gruffi Gummi. 1986 only. **$7.00.**

#7036 Walt Disney Gummi Bear Poseable Figures Grammi Gummi. 1986 only. **$7.00.**

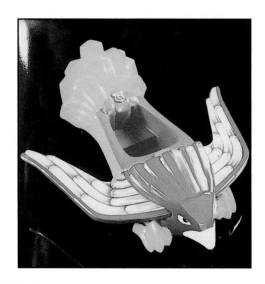

#7075 Walt Disney Gummi Bear Tunnel Eagle. 1986 only. Three-wheel eagle holds two poseable figures, makes screeching sound when pushed. Secret button springs wings open; wings move up and down. Eyes and beak glow in the dark. This toy was never produced for sale. **$20.00.**

#7050 Walt Disney Gummi Bear Puzzles. 1986 only. Nine different scenes. These puzzles made it to very few store shelves and are very rare finds. Titles are Zummi Gummi, Cubbi Gummi, Tummi Gummi, Sunni Gummi, Duke Igthorn and Ogre, Cavin and Calla, Grammi Gummi, Quick Tunnel, and Gruffi Gummi. **$25.00.**

Not pictured

#7100 Walt Disney Life-size Gummi Bear Plush Cubbi Gummi. 1986 only. Stuffed bears made with quality plush. 34" long x 20" high x 18" deep. Clothing is removable for dress-up fun. Character's biography and legend on back of each box. **$15.00.**

#7101 Walt Disney Life-size Gummi Bear Plush. Sunni Gummi. 1986 only. Same as #7100. **$15.00.**

#7076 Walt Disney Gummi Bear Bubble the Dragon. 1986 only. Vinyl dragon; when body is squeezed, bubbles fly out of his mouth. Head tilts back and eyes look down. Came with 4-oz. bubble solution. **$20.00.**

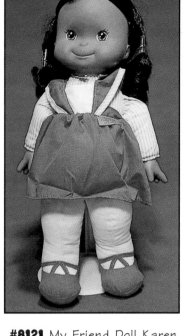

#8120 My Friend Doll Christie. 1990. This is a very hard doll to find due to a very short production run. **$40.00 – $75.00.**

#8121 My Friend Doll Karen. 1990. This doll was to be put in production but never made it; only 200 were made. **$100.00 – $175.00.**

#9516 Wood Toy Box. 1986 – 1988. This is an all-wood toy box. The lid is removable with a checkerboard printed on the top and the back side of toy box has a chalk board. The toy box measures 18½" high X 26½" wide and 17½" deep. **$300.00.**

1990 and Beyond

Although this book covers the past six decades of Fisher-Price toys, it is by no means the end of collectible toys as we know it. Because of the high volume of toys made from 1964 – 1990, a second book will be necessary to cover the large volume of toys not covered in this book, as well as the Little People sets and limited edition sets made after 1990. I am also starting to see a high demand for the Great Adventure sets. The sets pictured here are just a small sample of the post 1990 toys seeing a high demand: #2381 Chunky Fire Truck, #2356 Space Shuttle, #72549 Santa's Sleigh, #72654 Winter Wonderland, #72653 Christmas Surprise, and #72698 Christmas Train. A value and demand for the post 1990 toys have yet to be established.

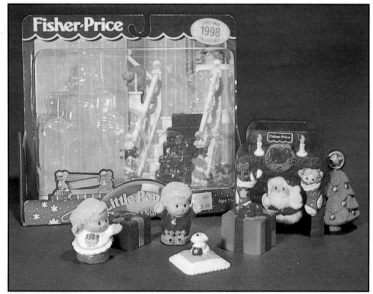

ToyFest Memorabilia

#6145 Jingle Elephant. 1993. ToyFest Limited Edition of 5,000. **$150.00.**

#6464 Gran'Pa Frog. 1994. ToyFest Limited Edition of 5,000. **$60.00.**

#6550 Buzzy Bee. 1987. ToyFest Limited Edition of 5,000. **$120.00.**

#6558 Snoopy. 1988. ToyFest Limited Edition of 3,000. **$550.00.**

#6575 Toot-Toot. 1989. ToyFest Limited Edition of 4,800. **$85.00.**

#6590 Prancing Horses. 1990. ToyFest Limited Edition of 5,000. **$75.00.**

#6592 Teddy Bear Parade. 1991. ToyFest Limited Edition of 5,000. **$75.00.**

#6599 Molly Bell Cow. 1992. ToyFest Limited Edition of 5,000. **$150.00.**

#6593 Squeaky the Clown. 1995. ToyFest Limited Edition of 5,000. **$150.00.**

This is a 5½ x 8½ card that was signed by Warren Hawkinson during ToyFest. He was one of the original artists of 1958 Squeaky. **$5.00.**

#76594 Woodsy-Wee Zoo. 1996. ToyFest Limited Edition of 5,000. **$125.00.**

#76880 Raggedy Ann & Andy. 1997. ToyFest Limited Edition of 5,000. The museum started making a limited run of 500 specialty boxes for their members. Museum members received their toy in a blue printed box; the regular boxes are printed in red. Although the only difference in the toy is the box, the member version commands a higher price on the secondary market. **$150.00.**

Signed by Joni Gruelle, daughter of the original designer of Raggedy Ann & Andy, Johnny Gruelle. **$200.00.**

#980750 Space Blazer. 1998. ToyFest Limited Edition of 5,000. The museum made a limited run of 500 specially made boxes for their members. Museum members received their toy in a black box with pink stars and the regular boxes are black with yellow stars. Although the only difference in the toy is the box, the member version commands a higher price on the secondary market. **$125.00.**

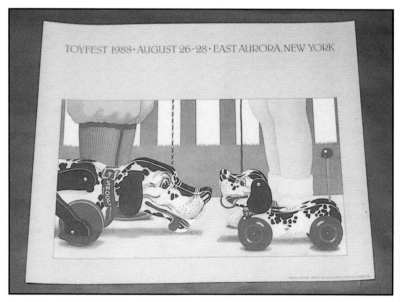

Snoopy Sniffer Poster. 1988. ToyFest Limited Edition of 3,000. **$17.00.**

Toot-Toot Poster. 1989. ToyFest Limited Edition of 5,000. **$44.00.**

Prancing Horses Poster. 1990.
ToyFest Limited Edition of 5,000.
$60.00.

Teddy Bear Parade Poster. 1991.
ToyFest Limited Edition of 5,000.
$17.00.

Molly Bell Cow Poster. 1992.
ToyFest Limited Edition of
5,000. **$17.00.**

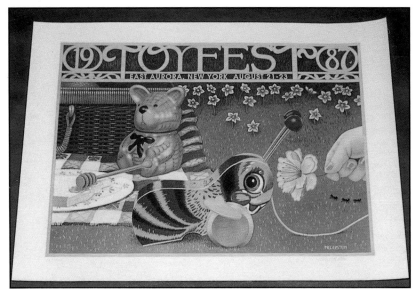

Buzzy Bee Poster. 1992. ToyFest Limited Edition of 5,000.
Note: In 1987 when the Buzzy Bee pull toy was made, there was not a poster to go with it, thus the 1992 date. **$12.00.**

Jingle Elephant Poster. 1993. ToyFest Limited Edition of 5,000. **$17.00.**

Gran'Pa Frog Poster. 1994. ToyFest Limited Edition of 5,000. **$12.00.**

Squeaky The Clown Poster. 1995. ToyFest Limited Edition of 5,000. **$12.00.**

Woodsy-Wee Zoo Poster. 1996. ToyFest Limited Edition of 5,000. **$16.00.**

Envelope and stamp set. 1993. This set of four circus postage stamps and envelope sets was sold only during ToyFest. **$45.00.**

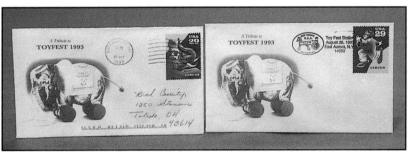

These key chains were given out at Fisher-Price Club dinners and sold at the Toy Town Museum. They are identical to the limited edition toys but have no numbers on the bottom. The Elephant was never made into a keychain.

Woodsy-Wee Zoo key chain Bear, very few made. **$35.00.**

Woodsy-Wee Zoo key chain Camel, second hardest to find. **$10.00.**

Woodsy-Wee Zoo key chain Lion, very common. **$10.00.**

Woodsy-Wee Zoo key chain Giraffe, very common. **$10.00.**

1931 Hawkeye Truck Bank. 1995 only. Limited edition of 500. The museum had this bank made up for the year of 1995 as a trial run. It was a complete sell-out. **$55.00.**

Not pictured

Hat and bandanna. 1989 only. An engineer's hat and red bandanna sold during ToyFest. **$15.00.**

1940 Coupe Bank. 1997 only. Limited edition of 1,250. The coupe is complete with color lithos showing each of the past 10 ToyFest toys and the 10th Anniversary ToyFest Logo. **$40.00.**

Plush Cow. 1992 only. A black and white plush cow with a bell around its neck sold during ToyFest. **$20.00.**

Sun Visor Hat. 1993 only. Blue sponge visor hat sold during ToyFest. **$8.00.**

Pogs. A set of 10 pogs with nine of them showing the first nine ToyFest Limited Edition toys. The 10th pog has the museum's logo. **$2.50.**

Lapel pins. Each pin shows one of the ToyFest limited edition toys. **$2.25 each.**

UNNUMBERED TOYFEST LOOK-ALIKE TOYS

The bee on the left is the unnumbered one and the one on the right is the numbered one.

As with any product run, extra toys are made to cover any loss that may occur, such as bad litho, paint, bandsawing, etc. Defective ones are destroyed, and the extra toys are used.

Normally all the extra toys are needed. These toys are identical and in perfect condition, except they have no number.

Many of the extra unnumbered toys were used as favors at business meetings sponsored by Fisher-Price and Quaker Oats in the Buffalo and Chicago areas. Some of the unnumbered toys were used for special programs in the plant, such as perfect attendance awards, productivity achievement, and picnic prizes. Trophies were also made from these toys for ToyFest events. These toys and even some of the unnumbered toys have been turning up at garage sales and flea markets.

The information below indicates approximately how many unnumbered toys are around and their selling prices.

#6550 1987 Buzzy Bee   200 toys, unnumbered   **$80.00 – $90.00**
#6558 1988 Snoopy Sniffer   300 toys, unnumbered   **$350.00 – $400.00**
#6575 1989 Toot-Toot   30 toys, unnumbered, no information
#6590 1990 Prancing Horses 50 toys, unnumbered, no information

Because of the small number of unnumbered toys in existence, some people believe they are as valuable or even more valuable than the numbered ones. I believe they are a rarity and a real find for any collection.

Another rarity is the "Prancing Horses," an extra 500 toys numbered 5001 through 5500 made with permission of the Chamber/ToyFest for the employees of the East Aurora factory. The East Aurora factory was closed in 1990. Each employee was given one of the specially-numbered toys when the factory closed. A sad day, but a nice keepsake. These toys show up occasionally and are a nice find and addition to a collection.

McDonald's Happy Meal Toys

These are items that came with a Happy Meal from McDonald's. There was no Fisher-Price Toy number assigned.

Record #1. 1985 only. Side A: Songs: "She'll be Comin' Round the Mountain," "Head, Shoulders, Knees, and Toes." Side B: Story: "The Object is Music." **$12.00.**

Record #3. 1985 only. Side A: Songs: "If You're Happy", "Little Bunny Foo Foo." Side B: Story: "The Ronald McDonald One-Man Band." **$12.00.**

Record #2. 1985 only. Side A: Songs: "Boom, Boom, Ain't It Great to be Crazy," "Do Your Ears Hang Low?" Side B: Story: "The Music Machine." **$12.00.**

Record #4. 1985 only. Side A: Songs: "Do The Hokey Pokey," "Ensy Weensy Spider." Side B: Story: "The Ronald McDonald Orchestra." **$12.00.**

Fun with Food Guys

Sets came with a set of eyes, McDonald's decals, and insert on Fisher-Price-made McDonald's line of toys.

1988 Set #1 Hamburger Guy. **$12.00.**

1988 Set #2 French Fry Guy. **$12.00.**

1988 Set #3 Soft Drink Guy. **$12.00.**

1988 Set #4 Chicken McNuggets Guys. **$12.00.**

Great Adventures Series-Knight. 1995 only. Black knight and green dragon. **$5.00.**

Once Upon A Dream Series. 1995 only. Princess figurine. **$5.00.**

McDonald's has made 48 different "Under 3" toys for the past year, selling on the secondhand market for **$2.00 each.**

MISCELLANEOUS TOYS

Amusement park boat with plastic girl figure made for the opening of the Medina Plant, April 14, 1971. **$20.00.**

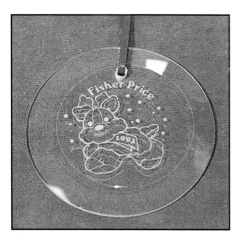

Christmas ornaments
These ornaments are made of glass with the art work etched on them. **$10.00 – $15.00 each.**

Cup Holder/Key Chain
Cup holder and chunky figure key chain were handed out to all the employees in the Murray, plant for the employee open house in 1996. **$5.00.**

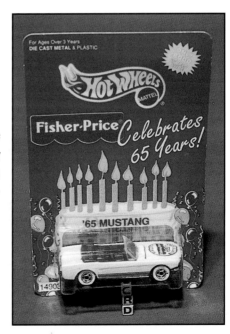

Henry Hippo
This item was either a mail-away or handed out at events such as Toy Fair. It was originally an infant toy made in 1978 – 1984 and numbered #625 Henry Hippo. A tub and pool toy, it floats like a hippo and also has wheels for floor play. When filled with water, he pours when tipped forward. He is pictured here as a pencil holder with this specially made box. MIB only. **$15.00.**

Hot Wheel
1995 only. Limited edition of 8,000. White Ford Mustang convertible with "Happy 65th Birthday Fisher-Price" on hood of car. This car was made for a company in Pennsylvania by Mattel. **$35.00.**

Juice Glasses
These were mail-away and have become very collectible. They sell anywhere from **$20.00 – $50.00 each,** depending on condition.

Key Chains
Around 1979 – 1980, Fisher-Price handed out key chains at Toy Fair made from common figures, the Indian and lady rancher from the Western town as well as Sesame Street figures, and provided them as favors at business meetings and promotional events. These are easy to fake; the only way to tell if one is real is by the attached Fisher-Price name tag as pictured. Common figures sell for around **$8.00 each** and the other figures sell for around **$15.00 each.**

The Sesame Street Character key chains pictured here in their boxes are a very true and rare find. As a matter of fact, I have only seen three of them in my 10 years of collecting. I know of no one who has ever seen them all. Because of this, there is no secondary market values. I would not sell one of mine for less than **$200.00.**

#932 Amusement Park. 1963 – 1965. Twenty play parts in all. Six big rides. Park map, chair ride, two cars, two boats, bridge/seesaw, musical merry-go-round, swing, four piece take-apart train, six straight body wood figures, two red, two green, two red or purple, and dog. **$300.00.**

#983 Safety School Bus. 1959 only. Four 3½" removable wood and litho figures. Bus has a removable wood lid. Stop sign swings out and door opens, eyes move, and driver looks side to side. Rear two figures bounce up and down and turn. Cool engine sound.

1960 & Easter 1961. The figures are now 2½" and all six are removable. **$250.00.**

#984 Safety School Bus. 1961 & Easter 1962. Driver looks left and right as bus rolls along with putt-putt-putt sound. Five wood figures, spring-hinged door, and swing-out stop sign. **$225.00.**

#6588 Snoopy Sniffer. 1990. Fisher-Price Commemorative Limited Edition of 3,500. This was the last toy made in E. Aurora plant; it is also the last toy made with Ponderosa pine. **$150.00.**

No number Doctor Doodle. 1980. Commemorative 50th Anniversary miniature Doctor Doodle 6¾" tall when neck is fully extended. **$325.00.**

#100 Doctor Doodle. 1995. Fisher-Price limited edition. This was advertised as First in a Series with only 5,000 being made. Has a wood body, plastic hardware, same litho and movements as the original. Also came with a mahogany base display stand. **$125.00.**

#234 Nifty Station Wagon. 1960 – 1962 & Easter 1963. Resembles a 1957 Chevy Wagon and has a removable roof, four wood figures, dad, mom, cone-shaped dog, and boy or girl. Headlight eyes roll around and the car roars brr-brum. **$250.00.**

#719 Fisher Price Choo-Choo Train. 1963 – 1966. Tilt-back engine cab and three cars. Three all-wood straight body figures in different colors, and dog. **$40.00.**

MARGARET EVANS PRICE MEMORABILIA

Books

1917 – 1935 Dates approximate by author. Margaret Evans Price illustrated and wrote children books. These books, like the paper dolls, have become very hot with both Fisher-Price collectors as well as children's book collectors. These books have gone for **$20.00 – $175.00** in very good condition.

Paper Dolls

1909 – 1931 Margaret Evans Price designed paper dolls which have become very hot and desirable for both Fisher-Price collectors and paper doll collectors. They range in price in very good condition from **$100.00 – $500.00.**

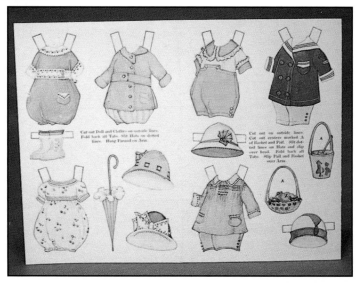

Postcards

Margaret Evans Price also designed and illustrated postcards for every occasion. These cards are a true find and can sell from **$10.00 — $50.00 each** in very good condition.

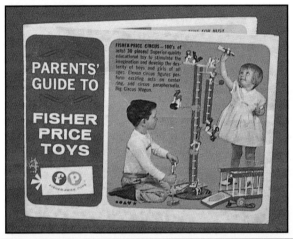

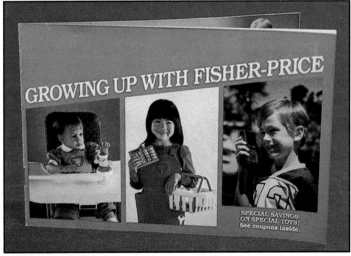

Pocket Catalogs

Fisher-Price put a small 4½ x 5½ pocket catalog in the box of every toy they sold to advertise their toy line. I do not know the exact year they started doing this other than the oldest pocket catalog I have ever seen is 1940. I also have no idea when they stopped doing this again other than by the newest catalog I have seen is 1985. These catalogs are very collectible and sell for a wide range of prices. The prices for the most part can be broken down by the decade.

1940 – 1949.	**$35.00.**
1950 – 1959.	**$30.00.**
1960 – 1969.	**$25.00.**
1970 – 1979.	**$20.00.**
1980 – 1985.	**$5.00.**

Whoops And Bits & Pieces

From time to time you will hear or see someone selling odd-colored bits and pieces, calling them a "whoops." This is the furthest thing from being true. If you have a glass of milk on a table and knock it over knowingly, do you say whoops? If you have a glass of milk on a table and knock it over by accident, do you say whoops? Most of us would not say whoops but a few other choice words. At any rate, if you do something knowingly, it is not a whoops, but if you had no intention to do it, that *is* a whoops. Any odd-colored pieces, such as purple moms, are simply cases of Fisher-Price using up discontinued parts. The purple moms are from the queen that went with the Castle. Fisher-Price would not throw out a few thousand bodies when they could use them with other sets. A true whoops is a figure having two collars, hair or hat on sideways, a female's body with a man's head, a mis-stamped face, etc.

Fisher-Price had also made odd-colored pieces like the blue ones pictured. No one has really been able to come up with a reason as to why they did this, but it was something done purposely.

No matter which one of these pieces you have, they are very collectible and highly sought after. I cannot put a value on any one piece, but I have seen these pieces sell from **$10.00 – $185.00 each.**

Not a whoops. Figures made by Fisher-Price employees just for fun.

A true whoops.

An odd-looking piece purposely made by Fisher-Price.

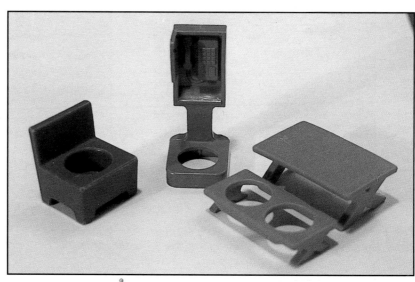

Zoo Series

The Toy Town Museum and the Buffalo Zoo announced a new line of antique toys manufactured locally, made available to the public in April 1998. The reproduction toys were made by All-Fair Toys and Games Company, long out of business, the company where Herman Fisher began his career.

The first toy is the All-Fair **#279** ABC Giraffe, recreated exactly as the original. The Giraffe is made of multi-colored beads for his neck and litho covered body celebrating the new arrival of the baby giraffe born at the Buffalo Zoo. The toy is also marked with the Toy Town Museum and Buffalo Zoo logos. The Giraffe is the first in a series of five limited edition toys they made and sold for **$85.00.** The Toy Town USA foundation presented the Buffalo Zoo with a check for $25,000, a portion of the proceeds from the ABC Giraffe.

Toy Town Museum and the Buffalo Zoo formed a partnership which includes membership discounts, joint programming, and a commitment to education, entertainment, and conservation of nature with the proceeds from the five replicas.

The second in the series of five All-Fair toys made, the camel was available to the public April of 1999 for **$85.00.** The reproduction is a Dromedary camel named Pebbles after the newest addition to the camel herd at the zoo.

ABC Giraffe. 1998.

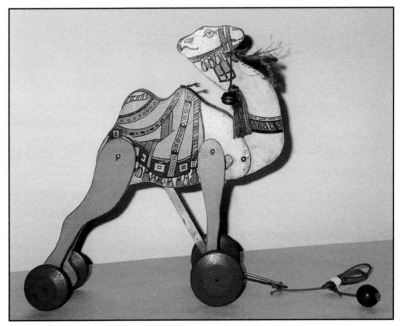

Pebbles the Camel. 1999.

FIGURES

One of the biggest questions asked about the Little People figures is when each different style of figures was made. This has always been a very controversial question. The dates here are to the year, give or take a few months, and any greater precision is not possible. The first removable figures are **#983** Safety School Bus Figures which are litho or paper covered and were produced through 1960. Although most people are not aware, there are two different styles of these figures. The first were 3" tall and made for only one year. After that they were only 2½" tall. The first bus had two prominently attached figures in the back of the bus but in late 1960 they were removable.

The **#234** Nifty Station wagon and **#168** Snorky Fire Engine were made from 1960 through the latter part of 1962. These are the first all wooden figures. This style of figure was also made for a new version of the Safety School Bus through the middle of 1965.

In 1960 Fisher-Price made smaller cylinder styled figure that were only 1½" tall and all wood. These figures came with such sets as the **#932** Amusement Park, **#719** FP Choo-Choo, **#979** DumpTrucker, and **#969** Music Box Ferris Wheel and were made until mid 1967.

In 1964 things start to get a little complicated. Fisher-Price started making new all-wood design figures that were no longer straight cylinder bodies even though they were still making the 1960 figures. These new figures were introduced with the **#192** School Bus and are probably the ones people remember the most. The bodies of these figures were still round but the lower section was smaller then the upper section so they could fit in furniture and cars. These new figures were made through early 1970 but not any later then 1972.

In 1970 Fisher-Price also started manufacturing the 1964 style figures but with plastic heads and wood bodies. These figures were made through 1974 but no later then 1975.

In 1971 Fisher-Price also started make these same figures of plastic.

In 1986 FP started making the Dads and Boys with molded hair and discontinued this whole line of figures in mid 1990.

In 1991 a new line of figures was introduced that was the same style as their predecessor, but twice the size and made of a softer plastic and soft rubber. The figures and playsets were still called Little People Play Sets but were safer for a younger age group.

The final change to the Little People figures was in 1997 when Fisher-Price introduced "Articular" figures made of soft rubber.

These two figures were introduced in 1971 and were made for the **#990** ATV Explorer. In 1975 they were also used with the Construction Trucks, a new line of toys.

It was not until 1984 that Fisher-Price started making different figures for infants. These set are **#136** Discovery Cottage and **#413** Shapes & Slides Playground. The Discovery Cottage is an oversized house and has 13 play features. It came with a tricycle, Lucky dog, and infant. The **#413** Shapes & Slides had three extra large Play Family Bears, one square, one round, and one triangle shaped for lots of learning and fun. The Floating Family was the longest lasting set, made through 1998.

These two tan/light brown Lucky dogs were made in 1965 and came with the **#192** School Bus or the **#663** Play Family Set. They are very rare and in high demand with no sight of dropping in value. **$30.00.**

Farm Animals

This listing is of all the different versions of the farm animals that I know. The names for the farm animals are Horace the Horse, Bossy the Cow, Spot the Dog, Pudgy Pig, Woolie Sheep, Rusty Rooster, and Henrietta Hen.

Horses: Rivet belly – No mark (USA), black horse, white eyes and mane. White horse, brown or black eyes, brown mane. Rivet belly w/ "Hong Kong" black or brown horse. Circle belly (no rivet), "Hong Kong," black or brown horse. Plain belly w/ "Hong Kong," shiny black, light brown or brown horse. Plain belly with "Taiwan" mark, shiny black or deep brown horse.

Cows: Rivet belly – No mark (USA), black cow, white spots; brown cow, white spots; and white cow, brown spots. Rivet belly with "Hong Kong," white cow, brown spots. Circle belly (no rivet), "Hong Kong," white cow, brown spots. Plain belly with "Hong Kong," shiny white cow, brown spots.

Sheep: Rivet belly – No mark (USA), black sheep, white eyes. Rivet belly – No mark (USA), white sheep, black ears, nose and legs. Rivet belly – "made in Hong Kong," white sheep, black eyes, ears, nose, and legs. Circle belly (no rivet) "made in Hong Kong", white sheep, black eyes, ears, nose, and legs. Circle belly (no rivet), "made in Hong Kong," bright white sheep, black eyes, nose, ears and legs. Circle belly (no rivet), "made in Taiwan," bright white sheep, black eyes, ears, nose, and legs.

Pigs: Rivet belly – No mark (USA), white pig, brown ears; brown pig, black ears. Rivet belly, "made in Hong Kong," black pig, light or dark gray ears. Circle belly, "made in Hong Kong," black pig, white ears. Smooth belly, "made in Hong Kong," pink pig, black eyes and nose; black pig, white ears, eyes, and nose.

Dogs: Rivet belly – No mark (USA), white dog, brown ears, eyes, nose and tail; black, white eyes, ears, nose, and tail; brown dog, dark brown ears, eyes, nose, tail, and one dark brown leg. Circle belly (no rivet), "made in Hong Kong," tan body or brown body, dark brown eyes, ears, nose with white spots on body. Smooth belly, tan body or shiny brown body dog, "made in Hong Kong," dark brown ears nose and tail with white spots on legs and body.

Chickens: Red rooster with black markings, shallow hole in bottom with "Hong Kong" on side or deeper hole in bottom with "Hong Kong" on bottom. White hen with red markings, shallow hole in bottom, "Hong Kong" on side, or deep hole in bottom with "Hong Kong" on bottom.

1931 – 1963
The Golden Years

#5 Bunny Cart. **$75.00.**
1948 – 1949. Bunny pulls a small round litho container with metal rim and bottom. Smaller in 1949. Easter only.

#6 Ducky Cart. **$75.00.**
1948 – 1949. Duck pulls a small round litho container with metal rim and bottom. Smaller in 1949. Easter only.

#7 Doggy Racer. **$200.00.**
1942 – 1943. Felt arms turn from side to side, makes roar sound when pulled.

#7 Looky Fire Truck. **$100.00.**
1950 – 1953 & Easter 1954. Eyes move up and down as bell rings when struck by wooden mallet. Firemen heads turn and bob up and down.

#8 Bouncy Racer. **$40.00.**
1960 – 1962. Helmeted driver's head and arms bounce up and down, makes a roar-roar sound when pulled. Metal roll bar behind driver's head. 1963 – 1972. Roll bar is omitted. **$30.00.**

#10 Bunny Cart. **$75.00.**
1940 – 1942. Bunny pulls a small round litho container with metal bottom.

#11 Ducky Cart. **$75.00**
1940 – 1942. Duck pulls a small round litho container with metal bottom.

#12 Bunny Truck. **$75.00**
1941 – 1942. Bunny pulls a small round litho container with metal bottom.

#14 Ducky Daddles. **$85.00.**
1941 Only. This is the mother duck from #799 Quacky Family.

#15 Bunny Cart. **$75.00.**
1946 – 1948 Bunny pulls a small round litho container with metal bottom.

#16 Ducky Cart. **$75.00**
1946 – 1948. Duck pulls a small round litho container with metal bottom.

#20 Animal Cut-Outs. **$50.00.**
1942 – 1946. Duck, Elephant, Pony, Scotty Dog. Price is per cut-out.

#22 Step 1 Blocks Set. **$40.00.**
1957 – 1971. Basic 22-piece set of wooden play blocks, made from pure Ponderosa pine, includes the following pieces: four square blocks, six basic units, two double units, two pillars, two small cylinders, four small triangles, one arch, and one half circle. All blocks have rounded edges, a natural wood finish, and a slightly napped surface texture that helps the blocks adhere to each other. Comes in 23" x 11½" x 1½" box.

#28 Bunny Egg Cart. **$75.00.**
1950 – 1951. Two-sided litho cart.

#22 Step 2 Blocks Set. **$45.00.**
1957 – 1971. Intermediate set consists of 41 pieces of various wooden assembly blocks. Contains eight square blocks, eight basic units, four double units, one quad unit, four half pillars, two pillars, two small cylinders, four small triangles, two arches, two half circles, and four small ramps. All blocks have rounded edges, a natural wood finish, and a slightly napped surface texture that helps the blocks adhere to each other. Comes in 23" x 11½" x 3" box.

#50 Baby Chick Tandem Cart. **$100.00.**
1953 – 1954. No toy number. Chick with two detachable carts.

#51 Ducky Cart. **$75.00.**
1950 only. Lithoed, two-sided.

#52 Rabbit Cart. **$75.00.**
1950 only. Lithoed, two-sided.

#75 Baby Duck Tandem Cart. **$100.00.**
1953 – 1954. No toy number Duckling with two detachable carts.

#100 Doctor Doodle. **$700.00.**
1931 only. Head bobs up and down with waddling motion. Bill opens and closes with quack sound.
1932 only. Same as above but with logo.
1933. New number (See #507).

#100 Musical Sweeper. **$100.00.**
1950 – 1952. "Disney." Working push sweeper plays "Whistle While You Work" when pushed across the floor.

#101 Granny Doodle. **$800.00.**
1931 – 1932. Head with felt bonnet bobs up and down with waddling motion. Bill opens and closes with quack sound.

#101 Granny Doodle & Family. **$850.00.**
1933 only. Head with felt bonnet bobs up and down, makes a quack sound as she waddles. Pulls two baby ducks attached with metal rods.

#102 Drummer Bear. **$700.00.**
1931 only. Arms beat drum and head bows.

#102 Drummer Bear. **$700.00.**
1932 – 1933. Fatter and taller than 1931.

#103 Barky Puppy. **$700.00.**
1931 – 1933. Oilcloth ears, pipe-cleaner tail with wooden ball. Crouches on his legs, tilting head up and down making barking sound.

#104 Lookee Monk. **$700.00.**
1931 only. Felt hat with tassel pipe-cleaner tail. Legs pedal as head turns side to side.

#105 Bunny Scoot. **$700.00.**
1931 only. Oilcloth ears; leg kicks as scooter rolls.

#109 Lucky Monk. **$700.00.**
1932 – 1933. Head and arms move up and down.

#110 Chubby Chief. **$700.00.**
1932 – 1933. Leg kicks and head with oilcloth hat bobs up and down ringing the bell.

#120 Gabby Goose. **$350.00.**
1936 – 1937 & Easter 1938. Head and neck glide back and forth as bill opens and closes, makes honk sound.

#120 Cackling Hen. **$40.00.**
1958 – 1966. White. Legs and wings move, makes a cluck-cluck-squawk sound.

#123 Roller Chime. **$50.00.**
1953 – 1960 & Easter 1961. Two clappers hit xylophone keys making melodious chimes.

#124 Roller Chime. **$35.00.**

1961 – 1962 & Easter 1963. Clapper hits xylophone keys making melodious chimes.

#125 Uncle Timmy Turtle. **$100.00.**
1956 – 1958. Red shell. Paddles legs and wags tail. Mallets hit keys in shell making musical sounds.

#131 Toy Wagon. **$225.00.**
1951 – 1954 Driver's head bobs up, down, and around. Prancing ponies and ringing bell.

#131 Music Box Sweeper. **$85.00.**
1961 – 1962 & Easter 1963. Swiss music box plays "This Is The Way We Sweep The Floor." Non working, unlike its predecessors.

#132 Doctor Doodle. **$85.00.**
1957 – 1960. Bill opens and closes, wings move up and down as tail wiggles, makes quack sound.

#137 Pony Chime. **$40.00.**
1962 – 1964 & Easter 1965. Ponies with wiggle spring tassels prance up and down pulling musical roller chime.

#139 Tuggy Turtle. **$100.00.**
1959 – 1960 & Easter 1961. Paddles his feet and wags his tail. Concealed xylophone keys.

#140 Coaster Boy. **$700.00.**
1941 only. Boy hops in and out of coaster and bell rings.

#140 Katy Kackler. **$85.00.**
1954 – 1956 & Easter 1957. Feet and wings move up and down while making cluck, cluck, cluck, squa-awk! cluck cluck noise.

#141 Snap-Quack. **$225.00.**
1947 – 1949. Head turns side to side and bill opens and closes making a quack-quack sound.

#145 Musical Elephant. **$225.00.**
1948 – 1950. Head turns from side to side, makes musical sounds.

#145 Husky Dump Truck. **$45.00.**
1961 – 1962 & Easter 1963. Dump lifts up, makes roar-roar sound. Figures bounce.

#145 Humpty Dump Truck. **$40.00.**
1963 – 1964 Easter 1965. Big polyethylene tires, cab, and grill. Bed dumps, makes roar-roar sound, round heads with wood nose.

#148 Ducky Daddles. **$225.00.**
1942 only. Turns head from side to side, has life-like moving webbed feet. Makes quack-quack sounds.

#148 Jack N Jill TV-Radio. **$75.00.**
1959 – Easter 1960. Retractable spring antenna, blue plastic face, and wood handle.
1960 – 1967. **$40.00.**
Retractable antenna omitted.

#149 Dog Cart Donald. **$700.00.**
1936 – 1937. Donald sits in driver's seat cracking the rubber whip over Pluto's waving tail. Pluto's legs race back and forth.

#150 Barky Buddy. **$600.00.**
1934 – 1935. Oilcloth ears, wood hat. Legs move, head tilts, makes loud woof-woof sound.

#150 Teddy Tooter. **$400.00.**
1940 – 1941. Rocks head and moves back and forth blowing toot-toot sounds.

#150 Timmy Turtle. **$100.00.**
1953 – 1955. Easter 1956. Green shell and red cap. Legs paddle, tail wags while making musical sounds.

#151 Happy Hippo. **$85.00.**
1962 – 1963. Mouth opens and closes to ho-ho-ho sound. Storage space inside hippo.

#152 Road Roller. **$700.00.**
1934 – 1935. Engineer leans back, pulling whistle lever.

#155 Skipper Sam. **$850.00.**
1934 only. Sam leans forward and back as rows. Makes a grunt sound with every stroke.

#155 Moo-oo Cow. **$85.00.**
1958 – 1961 & Easter 1962. Tosses head and makes moo-ooo sound. Tail swishes.

#156 Circus Wagon. **$400.00.**
1942 – 1944. Band leader moves his hands and arms as concealed piano wires are struck.

#159 Ten Little Indians TV-Radio. **$15.00.**
1961 – 1965 & Easter 1966. Wood case and handle with plastic face.

#160 Donald & Donna Duck. **$700.00.**
1937 only. Donald moves arms up and down striking keys, Donna swings arms and dances.

#160 Creative Block Wagon. **$75.00.**
1965 – 1966 (see #161).

#161 Looky Chug-Chug. **$250.00.**
1949 – 1952. Engine with tender car. Eyes look up and down as bell rings.

#161 Creative Block Wagon. **$75.00.**
1961 – 1964. Eighteen building blocks, six squares, six circles, six wedges, six wood dowels, all fit into a pull-along wagon.
1965 – 1966 numbered **#160.**

#166 Tumbling Tim. **$600.00.**
1939 only. 18" push stick. Moving arms and fold-back legs. Head moves back and rings bell ding-ding.

#166 Bucky Burro. **$250.00.**
1955 – 1957. Ears flip, spring tail swishes. Bucky bucks up and down making hee-haw sound.

#166 Farmer in the Dell TV-Radio. **$20.00.**
1963 – 1966. Wood case and handle with plastic face.

#168 Snorky Fire Engine. **$125.00.**
1960 & Easter 1961. Four green wood firemen and dog. Crank lifts snorkel and has a ringing bell. There are two versions of this toy. The words "Fisher-Price" can either be on the top of the boom or on the sides.

#169 Snorky Fire Engine. **$100.00.**
1961, Easter 1962. Red litho, four white wood firemen. Rotating snorkel lift raised up and down by crank. Ringing bell.

#170 American Airlines Flagship. **$700.00.**
1941 – 1942. Twin engine plane with plastic spinning propellers, whirring motor sounds.

#171 The Toy Wagon. **$300.00.**
1942 – 1947. Ponies prance up and down ringing bell.

#175 Kicking Donkey. **$450.00.**
1937 – 1938. Rear bounces up and down while making hee-haw sound. Rope tail and rubber ears.

#175 Gold Star Stagecoach. **$250.00.**

1954 – 1955. Easter 1956. Came with two wood litho mail pouches. Horses gallop making clippity clop sound as driver sways.

#177 Donald Duck Xylophone. **$300.00.**
1946 – 1952. Donald Duck is on the hat. Arms move up and down striking xylophone keys.

#180 Snoopy Sniffer. **$75.00.**
1938 – 1955. Fully jointed legs, makes woof-woof sounds. Spring-attached tail. Had oilcloth ears with rubber feet 1938 – 1939.

#180 Snoopy Sniffer. **$55.00.**
1958 – 1960. Easter 1961. Basset woof-woof-woof sound, leg action, and spring-attached tail with wood bead.

#181 Snoopy Sniffer. **$35.00.**
1961 – 1981. Woof-woof-woof sound, leg action, and spring-attached tail with wood bead.

#185 Donald Duck Xylophone. **$800.00.**
1938 – 1942. Marked WDE and WDP. The word "Donald Duck" is on bottom of litho by his feet. More if marked WDE. Moves arms up and down, striking xylophone keys.

#189 Looky Chug-Chug. **$85.00.**
1958 – 1960. Engine with tender car. Eyes look up and down, makes chug-chug sound.

#190 Gabby Duck. **$350.00.**
1939 – 1940 & Easter 1941. Moving legs with flapping feet. Bill opens and closes, makes a quack-quack sound.

#190 Molly Moo-Moo. **$225.00.**
1956 only, Easter 1957. Head moves up and down as ears twirl around making mooo sound. Spring attached tail with wood bead.

#191 Golden Gulch Express. **$100.00.**
1961 only. Easter 1962. Permanently attached miner car. Eyes roll up and down, pumping pistons, chug-chug sound.

#192 Playland Express. **$100.00.**
1962 & Easter 1963. Back door opens.

#195 Teddy Bear Parade. **$600.00.**
1938 only. Teddy bears' arm moves up and down. One bear beats drum, other is parade leader.

#198 The Band Wagon. **$350.00.**
1940 – 1941. Prancing ponies pull cart with music notes.

#200 Wheel Horse. **$500.00.**
1934 only. Riding horse with horsehair tail with red leather bridle.

#200 Winky Blinky Fire Truck. **$100.00.**
1954 – 1959. This was the beginning of the Little People. Eyes look up and down as bell rings. Firemen's heads turn and bounce.

#201 Woodsy-Wee Circus. **$750.00.**
1931 – 1932. Camel, elephant and baby, clown, dog, lion, monkey, giraffe, bear, pony, and flat cart. Each piece had a closed hook on one end and an open hook on the other to make a train.

#202 Woodsy Circus Wagon. **$2,000.00.**
1933 only. Break-down circus wagon with sides, end, and top. Giraffe, elephant, lion, camel, pony, and clown. Cardboard ticket booth and tickets. This set is extremely rare and has sold for $6,000.00 in mint condition.

#202a Woodsy Miniature Animals. **$85.00 each.**
1935 – 1937. Giraffe, horse, lion, clown, cow, camel, bear, monkey, dog, goat, pig, donkey, and elephant. These figures do not have hooks like Woodsy-Wee from 1931 and 1932.

#205 Woodsy-Wee Zoo. **$750.00.**
1931 – 1932. Camel, giraffe, lion, bear, and elephant with closed hooks on one end and open hooks on the other to make a train.

#205 Walt Disney's Parade
1936 – 1941. WDE. **$250.00 each.**
1941 WDP. **$100.00 each.**

#206a Walt Disney Characters. **$275.00.**
1936 – 1938. Mickey, Pluto, Donald, Elmer. Larger than #207a figures, 3" - 7".

#207 Woodsy-Wee Pets. **$650.00.**
1931. Goat, donkey, cow, pig, and cart with open and closed hooks.

#207a Walt Disney's Carnival. **$200.00 each.**
1936 – 1938. Mickey, Pluto, Donald, and Elmer. Smaller than #206a figures, 2" - 4"; same size as #483.

#208 Walt Disney's Donald Duck. **$175.00.**
1936 – 1938. Walt Disney. Donald Duck on small, beaded wooden wheels.

#209 Woodsy-Wee Dog Show. **$650.00.**
1932 only. St. Bernard, dachshund, collie, boxer, and Scotty with open and closed hooks.

#209 Walt Disney's Mickey Mouse. **$175.00.**
1936 – 1938. Mickey Mouse on small, beaded wooden wheels.

#210 Walt Disney's Pluto the Pup. **$175.00.**
1936 – 1938. Walt Disney. Pup on small, beaded wooden wheels.

#211 Elmer Elephant. **$175.00.**
1936 – 1938. Walt Disney. Elephant on small, beaded wooden wheels.

#215 Streamline Express. **$600.00.**
1935 only. Engine with eight wheels and ringing bell. Holds up to 150 pounds. All painted, no litho.

#215 Fisher Price Choo Choo. **$85.00.**
1955 – 1957. Engine with four cars connected with metal rods and choo-choo sound.

#220 Looky Chug-Chug. **$85.00.**
1953 – 1954 & Easter 1955. Engine and tender car. Bell rings with chug-chug sound.

#225 Wheel Horse. **$600.00.**
1935 & Easter 1936. Ride-on horse with red leather bridle and horsehair tail.

#225 Musical Sweeper. **$85.00.**
1953 – 1955 & Easter 1956. Makes musical sound and really works for helping mom.

#230 Musical Sweeper. **$85.00.**
1956 – 1957. Musical sweeper really sweeps.

#234 Nifty Station Wagon. **$250.00.**
1960 – 1962 & Easter 1963. Removable roof, four wood figures dad, mom, cone-shaped dog, and boy or girl. Rolls eyes and roars brr-brum.

#237 Riding Horse. **$600.00.**
1936 only. Riding horse with fiber tail with leather reins.

#244 Riding Horse. **$350.00.**

1941 – 1942. Can hold 500 pounds and has red leather reins.

#245 Riding Horse. **$350.00.**
1937 only. Larger than predecessors, with leather bridle and rope tail. Could hold the weight of three men.

#250 Big Performing Circus. **$950.00.**
1932 – 1938. Break-down wagon, ladder, ball, tub, merry-go-round, clown, giraffe, pony, bear, dog, camel, elephant, monkey, lion, and illustrated folder.

#254 Riding Horse. **$350.00.**
1940 only. Leather bridle.

#293 Riding Horse. **$550.00.**
1938 – 1939. Red leather bridle. Same as #5477.

#300 Quacko Duck. **$225.00.**
1939 – 1942. She wiggles, quacks, and jiggles.

#301 Bunny Basket Cart. **$40.00.**
1957 – 1959. Woven basket.

#301 Bunny Basket Cart. **$40.00.**
1960 only. Plastic basket.

#302 Chick Basket Cart. **$40.00.**
1957 – 1959.

#303 Bunny Push Cart. **$75.00.**
1957 only.

#303 Bunny Basket Cart. **$40.00.**
1960 – 1964. Lacy polyethylene basket.

#304 Running Bunny Cart. **$75.00.**
1957 only.

#304 Chick Basket Cart. **$40.00.**
1960 – 1964. Polyethylene basket.

#305 Walking Duck Cart. **$40.00.**
1957 – 1964. Feet rotate to a flippit-flop sound.

#306 Bizzy Bunny Cart. **$40.00.**
1957 – 1959.

#307 Bouncing Bunny Cart. **$40.00.**
1961 – 1963. Easter 1964. Hippety-hop, hippety-hop as head wiggles.

#309 Bunny Push Cart. **$40.00.**
1958 – 1960. Square wicker or round blue, yellow, or pink plastic basket.

#310 Mickey Mouse Puddle Jumper. **$125.00.**
1953 – 1955 & Easter 1956. Rear end of car sways. Mickey leans side to side, two litho versions.

#310 Rolling Bunny Basket. **$40.00.**
1961 – 1964. Easter basket, tote toy.

#311 Running Bunny Cart. **$40.00.**
1958 – 1959. Easter basket, tote toy.

#312 Running Bunny Cart. **$45.00.**
1960 – 1964. Roomy candy cart.

#314 Queen Buzzy Bee. **$40.00.**
1956 – 1958. Blue crown and yellow whirling wings, makes buzz-buzz sound.

#318 Bonny Bunny Wagon. **$40.00.**
1959 – 1961. Plastic cart and ringing bell.

#325 Buzzy Bee. **$40.00.**
1950 – 1956. First of four. Dark yellow and black litho, wheels and antennae are wood. Whirling wings and buzz-buzz sound.

#333 Butch the Pup. **$75.00.**
1951 – 1953 & Easter 1954. Swaggers along with wagging tail and gruff-gruff sound.

#345 Penelope the Performing Penguin. **$800.00.**
1935 only. Wind-up, walks up to 50 feet randomly backing up.

#350 Go'N Back Mule. **$900.00.**
1931 – 1933. Had oilcloth ears and rope tail with removable key. Wind-up, walks up to 50 feet randomly backing up.
1932 – 1933. **$800.00.**
    Same as earlier version except non-removable key and newly styled feet.

#355 Go'N Back Bruno. **$800.00.**
1931 only. Wind-up, walks up to 50 feet randomly backing up.

#358 Donald Duck Back Up. **$800.00.**
1936 only. Donald had hardboard wings connected with rubber swing as he angrily walks away. Wind-up, walks up to 50 feet randomly backing up.

#360 Go'N Back Jumbo. **$900.00.**
1931 – 1934. Oilcloth ears, rope tail, pipe-cleaner trunk with six wood beads, and removable keys. Wind-up, walks up to 50 feet randomly backing up.
1932 – 1934. Same as above except non-removable key and newly style feet.

#365 Puppy Back Up. **$800.00.**
1932 – 1936 Oilcloth ears and tongue, wooden tail, non-removable key, and newly style feet. Wind-up, walks up to 50 feet randomly backing up.

#369 Giant Snap-Lock Beads. **$100.00 each.**
1959. Plastic beads in five shapes, octagon, circle, round, oval, and accordion.

#375 Bruno Back Up. **$800.00.**
1932 only. Wind-up with non-removable key. Pushes three-wheeled wheelbarrow up to 50 feet randomly backing up.

#400 Tailspin Tabby.
1931 – 1938. Round cat made of wood beads, 50-lb. fishline, two rigs, oilcloth ears, and yellow painted face pop-up toy. Round paddle version very rare. **$250.00.**
Guitar. **$85.00.**

#400 Donald Duck Drum Major. **$275.00.**
1946 – 1948. Raises arms up and down, swinging baton.

#400 Donald Duck Drum Major Cart. **$275.00.**
1946 only. Arm swings baton.

#400 Chick Cart. **$80.00.**
1954 – 1956. Chick with spring flower litho.

#401 Push Bunny Cart. **$225.00.**
1942 only.

#401 Bunny Cart. **$80.00.**
1954 – 1956. Bunny with cart for Easter candy.

#402 Duck Cart. **$200.00.**
1943 only.

#404 Bunny Egg Cart. **$80.00.**
1949 only.

#405 Lofty Lizzy. **$225.00.**
1931 – 1933. Giraffe made of wood beads, 50-lb.

fishline, two rings, oilcloth ears on a guitar-shaped paddle pop-up Kritter.

#406 Bunny Cart. **$50.00.**
1950 – 1953.

#407 Dizzy Dino. **$225.00.**
1931 – 1932. Dinosaur pop-up Kritter.

#407 Chick Cart. **$50.00.**
1950 – 1953.

#410 Stoopy Stork. **$225.00.**
1931 – 1932. Stoopy Stork has hardboard feet, wood beads, and 50-lb. fishline pop-up Kritter on a round or guitar-shaped paddle.

#410 Sonny Duck Cart. **$225.00.**
1941 only.

#415 Lop Ear Looie. **$225.00.**
1934 only. Mouse pop-up Kritter made of wood beads and 50-lb. fishline.

#415 Super Jet. **$225.00.**
1952. Easter 1953. Pilot's head pivots around, makes a buzzing motor sound.

#420 Sunny Fish. **$225.00.**
1955 only. Spring mounted tail wiggles up and down, bell rings tinkle-tinkle.

#422 Jumbo Jitterbug. **$225.00.**
1940 only. Elephant pop-up Kritter.

#425 Donald Duck Pop-Up. **$400.00.**
1938 & Easter 1939. Mounted on a wood platform, beaded legs and neck move; has a rubber bill, oilcloth wings, and concealed voice.

#430 Buddy Bronc. **$350.00.**
1938 only. Rider bounces up and down to clip-clop sound.

#432 Mickey Mouse Choo Choo.
1938 – 1940 WDE. Lever action bell. **$600.00.**
1939 – 1940 WDP. **$550.00.**

#432 Donald Duck Drum Major. **$300.00.**
1948 – 1949. Also numbered 532.

#432 Donald Duck Drum Major Cart. **$300.00.**

1948 – 1950. Also numbered 532.

#433 Dizzy Donkey. **$125.00.**
1939 – 1942. Donkey pop-up Kritter with spring-attached tail.

#434 Ferdinand the Bull. **$600.00.**
1939 only. Legs move up and down, smells flowers.

#437 Waggy Woofy. **$225.00.**
1942 only. Waggy wig-wags making woof-woof sound. Spring-attached tail.

#440 Goofy Gertie. **$225.00.**
1935 only. Stork with hardboard feet made of wooden beads and 50-lb. fishline, pop-up Kritter.

#440 Pluto Pop-Up.
1936 – 1945. **$225.00.**
Oilcloth ears, wooden beads and 50-lb. fishline, marked WDE.
Marked WDP. **$100.00.**

#444 Fuzzy Fido. **$225.00.**
1941 – 1942. Waddles, spring-attached tail with wood bead.

#444 Puffy Engine. **$85.00.**
1951 – 1954. Moving piston-arms and puff-puff sound.

#444 Queen Buzzy Bee. **$40.00.**
1959 – 1961. Red litho whirling wings.

#444 Queen Buzzy Bee. **$10.00.**
1962 – 1985. Honeybee design litho.

#445 Hot Dog Wagon. **$250.00.**
1940 – 1941. Tail wags ringing bell.

#445 Nosey Pup. **$75.00.**
1956 – 1958 & Easter 1959. Hind legs waddle, makes sniff-sniff sound.

#446 Rainbow Stack. **$15.00.**
1960 – 1961, Easter 1962. Wood base with four plastic rings all the same size in blue, red, green, and orange.

#447 Woofy Wagger. **$85.00.**
1947 – 1948. Head swings side to side as he makes woof-woof sound. Spring-attached tail with wood bead.

#450 Kiltie Dog. **$400.00.**
1936 only. Only Scotty dog with wagging tail and woof sound.

#450 Donald Duck Choo Choo.
1940. 9½" long. **$400.00.**
Bell rings when pulled.
1941. 8½" long. **$400.00.**

#450 Donald Duck Choo Choo. **$200.00.**
1942 – 1945 & Easter 1949. Donald's hat is blue.

#450 Jolly Jumper. **$85.00.**
1954 – 1955. Legs flip-flop around rear, moving body up and down. Rolling eyes, makes croak-croak sound.

#454 Donald Duck Drummer. **$300.00.**
1949 – 1950. Arms with mallets that move up and down playing drum.

#455 Tailspin Tabby. **$85.00.**
1939 – 1942. Pop-up Kritter.

#456 Bunny & Container. **$225.00.**
1939 – 1940. Hopping motion and cart.

#460 Dapper Donald Duck. **$600.00.**
1936 – 1937. Hardboard waving wings, connected with rubber. Makes quack sound, has no number.

#460 Dapper Donald Duck. **$600.00.**
1938 only. New litho and no number. Wings swing as Donald makes quack-quack sound.

#460 Suzie Seal. **$40.00.**
1961 – 1963 & Easter 1964. Ball on nose spins and bounces, makes arf-arf sounds.

#461 Duck Cart. **$225.00.**
1938 – 1939. Litho duck on sturdy wood cart.

#462 Busy Bunny. **$200.00.**
1937 only. Bunny hops up and down.

#462 Barky. **$75.00.**
1958 – 1960. Eyes roll, makes woof sound.

#463 Donald Duck Drum Major or Cart. 1939. **$500.00.**
Also **#463-550** on the Drum Major and **#550** or **#463-550** on the Drum Major Cart. Both toys were marked WDE. Arms move up and down.

#464 Gran'pa Frog. **$85.00.**
1956 – 1958. Hippity hop motion with rolling eyes, makes a croak-croak sound.

#465 Teddy Choo-Choo. **$400.00.**
1937 only. Bell rings as train chugs.

#465 Woofy Wagger. **$75.00.**
1954 – 1955. Head swings side to side as he makes woof-woof sound. Spring-attached tail with wood bead.

#466 Busy Bunny Cart. **$75.00.**
1941 – 1941. Bunny hops up and down.

#469 Donald Cart. **$400.00.**
1940 only.

#469 Rooster Cart. **$400.00.**
1938 – 1940. Litho rooster with vibrating clank sound, round cardboard container with metal bottom and rim mounted on wood base.

#470 Tricky Tommy. **$350.00.**
1936 only. Cat push toy on 16" stick, swings paws together striking cymbals.

#470 Ducky Cart with Voice. **$350.00.**
1946 only. Makes quack-quack sound.

#472 Peter Bunny Cart. **$225.00.**
1939 – 1940. Arms with mallets move up and down striking bell.

#472 Jingle Giraffe. **$225.00.**
1956 only. Rings bell, has a spring-attached tail with wood bead.

#473 Merry Mutt. **$75.00.**
1949 – 1954 & Easter 1955. Merry Mutts' paws swing up and down striking keys.

#474 Bunny Racer. **$225.00.**
1942 only. Makes rumm-rumm sound.

#475 Walt Disney's Easter Parade. **$500.00.**
1936 – 1938. Donald Duck, Big and Little Bunny, Wee, Clara Cluck.

#476 Pop-Up Rooster. **$350.00.**
1936 only. Pop-up Kritter made of wood beads, 50-lb. fishline. Toy not pictured in catalog, even though it was made.

#476 Mickey Mouse Drummer. **$300.00.**
1941 – 1945 & Easter 1946. Arms move up and down striking drum, rat-a-tat-tat.

#477 Doctor Doodle. **$225.00.**
1940 – 1941. Waddles, bill opens and closes with quack-quack sound.

#478 Pudgy Pig. **$50.00.**
1962 – 1964 & Easter 1965. Tail twirls, makes oink-oink-oink sound.

#479 Donald Duck & Nephews. **$400.00.**
1941 – 1942. Donald quacks as Huey and Louie balance swaying parasols.

#479 Peter Pig. **$45.00.**
1959 – 1961 & Easter 1962. Tail spins round and round to an oink-oink sound.

#480 Teddy Station Wagon. **$225.00.**
1942 only. Bears arms move up and down striking colored bell.

#480 Leo the Drummer. **$225.00.**
1952 & Easter 1953. Lion's paws move up and down striking drum.

#483 Walt Disney's Carnival. **$600.00.**
1936 – 1937. Mickey, Pluto, Donald, and Elmer Folding display box becomes the Big Top tent and the deck becomes the stage or chute. Set included a wood pedestal.

#485 Mickey Mouse Choo Choo. **$100.00.**
1949 – 1954 New litho version of #432. Bell rings automatically ding, ding, ding.

#487 Bunny Cart. **$225.00.**
1938 – 1939. No bell. Litho bunny on cart.

#487 Bunny Cart. **$225.00.**
1938 only. Bunny with cart, bell moves up and down.

#488 Popeye Spinach Eater. **$600.00.**
1939 – 1940. Arms with mallets move up and down striking spinach can.

#490 Easter Bunny. **$225.00.**
1936 only. Wood painted bunny cut-out.

#491 Boom Boom Popeye. **$450.00.**
1937 – 1938. Arms move up and down striking drum.

#494 Pinocchio. **$600.00.**
1939 – 1940. Pinocchio rocks back and forth striking bell.

#495 Running Bunny Cart. **$225.00.**
1941 only. Bunny pulling wood cart.

#495 Sleepy Sue Turtle. **$45.00.**
1962 – 1963 & Easter 1964. Blue hat and white shell with red dots. Tail wags, makes a snooze-snooze sound.

#496 Tiny Tim. **$40.00.**
1957 – 1961 & Easter 1962. Tail wags, makes chuck-chuckles sounds.

#498 Happy Helicopter. **$225.00.**
1953 – 1954 & Easter 1955. Propeller whirls with buzz-buzz sound.

#499 Kitty Bell. **$125.00.**
1950 – 1951. Kitty's arms move up and down playing with spinning wood ball as bell rings.

#500 Pushy Pig. **$500.00.**
1932 – 1935. 18" stick. Legs gallop and arms swing. Makes a squeal sound as head bobs.

#500 Donald Duck Cart. **$700.00.**
1937. No toy number. Arms swing. Wheels not painted on this toy.

#500 Donald Duck Cart. **$350.00.**
1951 – 1953. Without baton, green litho background and in 1953 a new litho was used with yellow background.

#502 Action Bunny Cart. **$200.00.**
1949 only. Bunny with rocking head and ears mounted on wooden base with cart.

#505 Bunny Drummer. **$225.00.**
1946 only. Bell on front of cart. Arms move up and down striking bell.

#505 Bunny Drummer. **$225.00.**
1947 only. Bunny swings arms holding mallets. Bell on top of cart.

#505 Bunny Drummer **$225.00.**
1948 only. Bell inside cart.

#507 Pushy Doodle. **$850.00.**

1933 only. Same as #100 Dr. Doodle, but with 18" stick.

#508 Bunny Bell Drummer. **$85.00.**
1949 – 1953. Same as above, blue or red cart.

#510 Strutter Donald Duck. **$250.00.**
1941 only. Arms swing back and forth, makes quack-quack sound.

#512 Bunny Drummer. **$225.00.**
1942 only. Paws move up and down striking bell.

#515 Pushy Pat. **$550.00.**
1933 – 1935. 18" stick. Arm tugs bell.

#517 Choo-Choo Local. **$550.00.**
1936 only. 18" stick. Dog paw tugs bell.

#520 Pushy Drummer. **$650.00.**
1934 only. Separately operated snare drum action and noise. Pull the ring and drummer beats snare drum roll. When pushed with 18" adjustable stick, he marches.

#520 Bunny Bell Cart. **$225.00.**
1941 only. Paws with mallets strike bell.

#525 Pushy Elephant. **$550.00.**
1934 – 1935. 18" stick. Beats cymbals together as legs beat on base for clang-clang sound.

#525 Cotton Tail Cart. **$350.00.**
1940 only. Legs move with walking motion, makes click sound.

#530 Mickey Mouse Band. **$800.00.**
1935 – 1936. Arms move up and down striking drum and cymbal on Pluto's tail. 18" push stick.

#533 Thumper Bunny. **$500.00.**
1942 only. Tail wags hitting painted bell.

#540 Granny Duck. **$225.00.**
1939 – 1940. Head turns left and right, makes quack-quack sound when pulled.

#540 Granny Duck. **$225.00.**
1941 – 1942. New litho design, stationary head, no sound. Listed as #545 on order forms.

#544 Donald Duck Cart. **$300.00.**
1942 – 1944. Arms move up and down, quacks when pulled.

#545 Granny Duck. **$225.00.**
1939 only. Same as #540, except stationary head, no sound.

#549 Toy Lunch Kit. **$25.00.**
1962 – 1979. Plastic lunch box with barn-style litho. Blue silo thermos fits inside.

#550 Donald Duck Drum Major and
Donald Duck Drum Major Cart. **$300.00.**
1940. Was also **#463** and marked WDE. Donald rocks back and forth flapping arms

#550 Toy Lunch Kit. **$40.00.**
1957 – 1961 & Easter 1962. Has the same shape as the barn lunch box, but with no litho, red and white.

#600 Woodsy Cart. **$1,200.00.**
1932 only. Total of six styles pulled by dog, clown, bear, elephant, lion or pony. Riders made of pipe-cleaners and wooden beads and are the first people figures Fisher-Price made. Extremely rare toys. Price listed is starting price.

#600 Tailspin Tabby Pop-Up. **$250.00.**
1947 only. Wooden beaded tabby moves when a wood disk is pushed.

#604 Bunny Bell Cart. **$100.00.**
1954 – 1955. Bunny paws swing up and down striking bell. Flowered litho cart.

#605 Horse And Wagon. **$600.00.**
1933 only. Realistic leg action and cart.

#605 Donald Duck Cart. **$300.00.**
1954 – 1956. Donald with Easter cart, flip-flop feet, quack-quack sound.

#610 Horse & Wagon and Blocks. **$600.00.**
1934 – 1935. Striding horse with wagon.

#610 Tailspin Tabby. **$85.00.**
1948 – 1949. Cat pops up.

#615 Tow Truck. **$75.00.**
1960 – 1961 & Easter 1962. Manually working hook, driver bounces and looks around, clatter-clack engine sound.

#616 Chuggy Pop-Up. **$100.00.**
1955 – 1956. Engineer pops up and down, chug-chug sound.

#616 Patch Pony. **$50.00.**
1963 – 1964 & Easter 1965. Pony has up and down motion tossing around spring-mounted head and tail, clippity-clop sound.

#617 Whistling Engine. **$100.00.**
1957 & Easter 1958. Bear litho. Fiber boiler with metal cap moves back and forth in pumping motion making whistle sound.
1958 & Easter 1959. **$85.00.**
New litho, jagged looking pattern

#625 Playful Puppy. **$50.00.**
1961- 1962 & Easter 1963. Grr-rrs and tosses head side to side, shaking plastic shoe.

#626 Playful Puppy. **$50.00.**
1963 – 1965 & Easter 1966. Grr-rrs and tosses head side to side, shaking plastic shoe.

#627 Rock-A-Stack. **$15.00.**
1960 – 1987. Wooden base through 1966. Rings fit on cone in spectrum order.
1960 – 1979. **$8.00.**
Had six rings.
1980 – 1987. **$2.00.**
Had five rings.

#629 Fisher Price Tractor. **$30.00.**
1962 – 1968. Bumpity-bumps with swaying boy, roar-roar engine sound.

#630 Fire Truck. **$50.00.**
1959 – 1962. Driver's head turns and bounces, makes roar-roar sound. Two-piece ladder extends.

#633 Creative Blocks. **$5.00.**
1963 only. Nine smooth rounded plastic blocks in six different colors, three each square, circle, and wedge, and two wooden dowels.
1964 – 1977. **$5.00.**
Same as above but with four wedge blocks instead of three.

#634 Tiny Teddy. **$75.00.**
1955 – 1957. Paws swing up and down with spring-mounted mallets striking three keys.

#635 Tiny Teddy. **$40.00.**

1962 – 1966. Swings mallet striking three keys.

#636 Tiny Teddy. **$55.00.**
1958 – 1961. Teddy candy man swings mallets striking three keys.

#640 Wiggily Woofer. **$85.00.**
1957 & Easter 1958. Head turns and tilts, ears wiggle up and down. Spring-mounted tail, makes woof-woof-woof sound.

#641 Toot Toot Engine. **$60.00.**
1962 – 1963 & Easter 1964. Blue litho steam engine with chug sound and piston action.

#642 Dinky Engine. **$60.00.**
1959 only. Black litho, chug-chug sound, piston action.

#642 Smokie Engine. **$75.00.**
1960 – 1961 & Easter 1962. Black litho, chug-chug sound, piston action.

#649 Stake Truck. **$50.00.**
1960 – 1961 & Easter 1962. Driver bounces and turns head, truck makes putt-putt-putt sound.

#653 Allie Gator. **$100.00.**
1960 – 1961 & Easter 1962. Flippers rotate on wheels as he wobbles along. Makes gobble-gobble sound.

#654 Tawny Tiger. **$100.00.**
1962 & Easter 1963. Shakes head, makes purr-purr-purrs sound. Vinyl tail and ears.

#656 Bossy Bell. **$60.00.**
1959 & Easter 1960 without bonnet. Tail spins around and bell rings.

#656 Bossy Bell. **$60.00.**
1960 & Easter 1961 with green plastic bonnet. Tail spins around and bell rings.

#656 Bossy Bell. **$50.00.**
1961 – 1963. No bonnet and new litho. Tail spins around and bell swings.

#658 Giant Snap-Lock Beads. **$1.00 each.**
1958 only. Fifteen beads in the box. Three shapes, oval, round, and cylinder. Six colors, dark blue, light blue, yellow, orange, red, and green.

#658 Lady Bug. **$55.00.**
1961 – 1962 & Easter 1963. Whirling shell and twirp-twirp sound. Spring antennae.

#662 Merry Mousewife. **$50.00.**
1962 – 1964 & Easter 1965. Sweeps broom side to side with squeak-squeak sound.

#674 Sports Car. **$85.00.**
1958 – 1960. Another of the Little People beginners. Pink, red, blue, and black cars with or without various designs painted on sides of cars. Cars make roaring sound.

#678 Kriss Kricket. **$100.00.**
1955 – 1957. Rear legs move body up and down in jumping motion with chirp-chirp.

#682 Rattle Ball. **$8.00.**
1959 – 1987. Wooden ball inside a gold-flecked acetate ball with 17" push stick and plastic safety knob on end.

#686 Perky Pot. **$50.00.**
1958 – 1959 & Easter 1960. Turn crank and ball strikes dome making pop-pop sound.

#695 Pinky Pig. **$100.00.**
1956 – 1957. Wood eyes, spinning umbrella, and oink-oink sound. Newer version had litho eyes.

#698 Talky Parrot. **$100.00.**
1963 & Easter 1964. Whirling wings with squawk-squawk sound. Plastic tail feathers.

#700 Popeye. **$700.00.**
1935 only. Popeye swings arms, hitting bell.

#700 Woofy Wowser. **$400.00.**
1940 & Easter 1941. Big rubber tail. Moving legs, makes woof-woof sound.

#700 Cowboy Chime. **$250.00.**
1951 – 1953. Pony's head on stick attached to musical canister.

#703 Popeye the Sailor. **$700.00.**
1936 only. Arms swing side to side ringing bell.

#703 Bunny Engine. **$100.00.**
1954 – 1956. Bunny engineer with flower-decked tender, rings bell.

#705 Racing Pony. **$550.00.**
1933 only. Realistic leg action and multiple painted number on saddle. Click-click-click sound.

#705 Popeye Cowboy. **$700.00.**
1937 only. Popeye on horse bounces up and down. Rope tail on horse.

#707 Fido Zilo. **$85.00.**
1955 – 1957 & Easter 1958. Xylophone pivots as paws swing up and down with spring-mounted mallets striking keys.

#710 Scotty Dog. **$550.00.**
1933 only. Realistic leg action.

#711 Raggedy Ann & Andy. **$850.00.**
1941 only. Their arms with mallet move up and down taking turns striking can.

#711 Teddy Trucker. **$225.00.**
1949 – 1951. Working tail gate and arms move up and down striking bell.

#711 Huckleberry Hound Zilo. **$300.00.**
1961 only. Sears only. Four key pivoting xylophone with springy wood mallets.

#712 Johnny Jumbo. **$550.00.**
1933 – 1935. Bobs frantically ringing his bell.

#712 Teddy Tooter. **$250.00.**
1957 – 1958 & Easter 1959. Nods head up and down, makes toot-toot-toot sound.

#712 Fred Flintstone Zilo. **$250.00.**
1962 only. Sears only. Three-key pivoting xylophone with springy wood mallets.

#714 Mickey Mouse Zilo. **$275.00.**
1963 only. Sears only. Three-key pivoting xylophone with springy wood mallets.

#715 Donald Duck Delivery. **$600.00.**
1936 only. No toy number. Swings arms.

#715 Peter Bunny Engine. **$225.00.**
1941 – 1944. Six-wheeled engine with an open tender car and ringing bell.

#717 Ducky Flip Flap. **$400.00.**
1937 – 1939. Duck has flapping rubber feet, leatherette wings, and quack sound. Pulls wooden cart.

#719 Busy Bunny Cart. **$350.00.**
1936 – 1937. Bunny and cart are painted.

#719 Fisher Price Choo-Choo Train. **$40.00.**
1963 – 1966. Tilt-back engine cab and three cars. Three all-wood straight body figures in different colors, and dog.

#720 Pinocchio Express. **$500.00.**
1939 – 1940. Legs move up and down to a vibrating sound.

#721 Peter Bunny Engine. **$200.00.**
1949 – 1951. Ringing bell, six-wheeled engine.

#722 Racing Bunny Cart. **$350.00.**
1937 only. Litho bunny.

#722 Running Bunny. **$225.00.**
1938 – 1940. Bunnies hop up and down.

#722 Musical Push Chime. **$40.00.**
1950 – 1952. 7¾" w. Metal cylinder with nursery rhyme printing and 18½" removable push stick. Rolls making music.
1953 – 1967. 8½" w. **$40.00.**

#723 Bouncing Bunny Cart. **$350.00.**
1936 only. Bouncing bunny pushes cart.

#723 Racing Bunny Cart. **$350.00.**
1938 – 1939. Litho bunnies pull wood cart back and forth ringing bell.

#724 Ding-Dong Ducky. **$225.00.**
1949 – 1950. Head turns from side to side as concealed piano wires play a tune.

#725 Musical Mutt. **$350.00.**
1935 – 1936. Mutt pulls big wheel with three bells.

#727 Bouncing Bunny Cart. **$350.00.**
1938 only. Bell on neck, bunny bounces while pushing cart.

#727 Bouncing Bunny Wheelbarrow. **$350.00.**
1939 only. Bell on head rings as bunny hops up and down, pushing wheelbarrow.

#728 Buddy Bullfrog. **$75.00**
1959 – 1960. Yellow body with red coat litho. Jumping action and croaking, grump-grump sound.

1961 only. **$75.00.**
Green coat with red and white pants litho.

#730 Tabby Ding Dong. **$350.00.**
1939 only. Arms move tugging on bell.

#730 Racing Rowboat. **$200.00.**
1952 – 1953. Rows as figure leans back and forward.

#733 Pony Express. **$225.00.**
1941 – 1944. Horse gallops and head bobs up and down arching his back. Rear quarter moves up and down, making clip-clop sound.

#733 Mickey Mouse Safety Patrol. **$250.00.**
1956 – 1957. Arms move signs up and down, one reading "STOP," the other "GO." Makes siren sound wee-eeeee.

#735 Juggling Jumbo. **$225.00.**
1958 – 1959. Turn crank and five wooden balls pop through his trunk.

#737 Galloping Horse & Wagon. **$250.00.**
1948 – 1949. Horse gallops and head bobs up and down arching his back. Rear quarter moves up and down, making clip-clop sound.

#737 Ziggy Zilo. **$75.00.**
1958 – 1959. Base zigs and zags as mallets hit four xylophone keys.

#738 Dumbo Circus Racer. **$700.00.**
1941 & Easter 1942. Rubber arms connected to steering wheel move back and forth as car makes roar sound when pulled.

#738 Shaggy Zilo. **$75.00.**
1960 – 1961 & Easter 1962. Pivoting xylophone key and paws move up and down, striking xylophone keys.

#739 Poodle Zilo. **$75.00.**
1962 – 1963 & Easter 1964. Three-key pivoting xylophone with wood mallets.

#740 Pushcart Pete. **$600.00.**
1936 – 1967. As Pete pushes a cart, his legs and head move. This toy had no litho, but was painted.

#740 Giant Rock-A-Stack. **$20.00.**
1961 – 1988. Wooden base through 1967. Rings fit on removable cone in spectrum order.

1961 – 1979. **$10.00.**
   Ten rings.
1980 – 1987.
   Seven rings. **$2.00.**

#741 Trotting Donald Duck. **$800.00.**
   1937 only. A #358 look-alike. Running action and quack-quack sound, Donald pulls cart.

#742 Dashing Dobbin. **$350.00.**
   1938 – 1940. 17" braided bridle.

#744 Doughboy Donald. **$600.00.**
   1942 only. Head moves up and down as Donald bounces back and forth on cart making loud quack-quack sound.

#745 Elsie's Dairy Truck. **$700.00.**
   1948 – 1949. Two bottles numbered on bottom 1 and 2. Cow's legs move up and down striking bell.

#747 Talk-Back Telephone. **$75.00.**
   1961 & Easter 1962. Voice sounds talk-a-talk-a-talk, and eyes roll up and down when pulled. Bell rings when dialed.

#747 Chatter Telephone. **$40.00.**
   1962 – 1987. Wooden wheel till 1967. This price is for phone with wood wheels only.

#749 Egg Truck. **$225.00.**
   1947 only. Felt arms turn steering wheel, engine sounds.

#750 Hot Dog Wagon. **$400.00.**
   1938 only. Paws with mallets move up and down, striking bell.

#750 Space Blazer. **$400.00.**
   1953 – 1954. Spinning saucer with dome and green man from Mars. Bell rings, has spring-attached antenna with wood bead.

#751 Giant Snap Lock Beads. **$1.00 each.**
   1959. Thirty-two beads in eight colors and five shapes.

#752 Teddy Zilo. **$350.00.**
   1946 – 1947. First version. Teddy has clown outfit and red cheeks. Paws with mallets move up and down, striking xylophone keys.

#752 Teddy Zilo. **$325.00.**

1948 – 1949 & Easter 1950. Outfit omitted from litho. Arms with mallet move, hitting xylophone.

#752 Giant Snap-Lock Beads. **$1.00 each.**
   1960 – 1968. 38 plastic beads in five shapes, octagon, circle, round, oval, and accordion.

#755 Jumbo Rolo. **$225.00.**
   1951 – 1952. Jumbo Rolo pedals his tricycle and wooden balls rattle in cage.

#757 Howdy Bunny. **$350.00.**
   1939 – 1940. Running legs and rubber ears.

#757 Snappy-Quacky. **$225.00.**
   1950 only. Head turns side to side and bill opens and closes making a quack sound.

#757 Humpty Dumpty. **$200.00.**
   1957 & Easter 1958. Eyes, arms, button, and feet revolve, bell rings.

#757 Melody Push Chime. **$15.00.**
   1963 – 1990. Metal cylinder with polyethylene tires, yoke, and safety knob on wooden push stick.

#758 Pony Chime. **$200.00.**
   1948 – 1950. Musical drum, wooden litho horse.

#760 Racing Ponies. **$350.00.**
   1936 only. Prancing ponies race with bells.

#760 Snap-Lock Beads. **$1.00 each.**
   1957. Beads in five shapes, octagon, circle, round, oval, and accordion.

#763 Farmer-In-Dell Music Box. **$50.00.**
   1962. Yellow litho. Turn crank to play, 26" vinyl neck strap.

#764 Hot Dog Wagon. **$350.00.**
   1939 only. Paws with mallets move up and down, striking bell.

#764 Farmer-In-Dell Music Box. **$50.00.**
   1960 – 1961 & Easter 1962. Red litho. Turn crank to play music. Has 26" vinyl strap.

#765 Dandy Dobbin. **$200.00.**
   1941 – 1944. Litho horse with braided cord bridle. Holds up to 150 pounds.

#765 Talking Donald Duck. **$125.00.**

1955 – 1958. Makes quack-quack sound. Arms swing up and down as feet paddle.

#766 Prancing Horses. **$400.00.**
1937 – 1938. New design of #760. Jockeys ride two prancing ponies with ringing bells.

#767 Tiny Ding-Dong. **$400.00**
1940. Had six wheels. Elephant engineer's arms tug bell.
1941. **$400.00.**
    Had four wheels.

#767 Gabby Duck. **$85.00.**
1952 – 1953. Waddling motion and bill opens and closes to a quack-quack sound.

#770 Doc & Dopey Dwarfs. **$1,000.00.**
1938 only. Doc's and Dopey's arms move up and down taking turns hitting stump.

#770 Dopey Dwarf. **$750.00.**
1939 only. Arms with mallets move up and down, striking stump.

#771 Creative Blocks. **N/A**
1961 – 1977. Eighteen smooth, rounded building blocks in six colors; six each, circles, squares, and wedges, fit over six wood dowels.

#773 Tip-Toe Turtle. **$15.00.**
1962 – 1977. Plastic shell with wood body. Makes music when pulled and feet rotate. First came with wooden wheels then plastic in the mid 1970s.

#775 Teddy Drummer. **$675.00.**
1936 only. Arms move up and down, one striking drum, other striking cymbal.

#775 Gabby Goofies. **$45.00.**
1956 – 1959 & Easter 1960. Wood hat and no collar. Daddy chatter-chatters as family waddles, spinning their wings.

#776 Gabby Goofies. **$40.00.**
1960 – 1962 & Easter 1963. Mama with vinyl and wood hat chatter-chatters as family waddles, spinning their wings.

#777 Pushy Bruno. **$725.00.**
1933 only. 18" stick. Legs stride along as right arm rings bell, wooden parasol.

#777 Pushy Bruno. **$550.00.**
1934 – 1935. 18" stick and wood parasol moves up and down with arms.

#777 Teddy Bear Zilo. **$75.00.**
1950 – 1954. Arms move up and down.

#777 Squeaky the Clown. **$250.00.**
1958 – 1959. Head moves up and down, makes squeak-squeak sound.

#777 Gabby Goofies. **$25.00.**
1963 – 1970. Mama with new style hat and color.

#778 Ice Cream Wagon. **$350.00.**
1940 & Easter 1941. Paws move up and down striking bell. Top swings open.

#780 Jumbo Xylophone. **$275.00.**
1937 – 1938. Arms move up and down, striking five keys.

#780 Snoopy Sniffer. **$75.00.**
1955 – 1957 & Easter 1958. Vinyl paws and ears, spring-attached tail, makes woof-woof sound.

#784 Mother Goose Music Cart. **$100.00.**
1955 – 1956 & Easter 1957. Flip-flop feet and three concealed xylophone keys; pulls cart.

#785 Blackie Drummer. **$625.00.**
1939 only. Swinging arm hits drum and raising arm clashes the cymbal.

#785 Corn Popper. **$75.00.**
1957 – 1958. Red base with blue wooden wheels, 14 multicolored wooden balls, and gold-flecked dome.
1959 – 1963. **$60.00.**
    White base with blue wooden wheels, 14 multi-colored wooden balls, and gold-flecked dome.

#787 Crib Rattle. **$15.00.**
1960 – 1961. Spinning gold-flecked glob with rattle-rattle sound. Vinyl removable straps for roller play.

#788 Rock-A-Bye Bunny Cart. **$300.00.**
1940 – 1941. Jointed arms rock cart with click-click sound.

#788 Corn Popper. **$10.00.**
1963 – 1987. White corn popper with 14 wood balls, plastic wheels, and gold-flecked dome. Later the balls were made of plastic.

#793 Jolly Jumper. **$50.00.**
　　1963 – 1964 & Easter 1965. Polyethylene rear wheels, mouth opens and closes to a loud croak sound. Has a red plastic hat.

#794 Big Bill Pelican. **$85.00.**
　　1961 – 1963. Large polyethylene bill opens and closes, flipper-like feet rotate with paddling motion. Solid wood body with vinyl head feathers. Makes a crew-aww sound and came with cardboard fish.
　　1964 – 1968. **$60.00.**
　　　　Fish was omitted.

#795 Mickey Mouse Drummer. **$700.00.**
　　1937 only. Pie-eyed, arms move, one striking drum, other the cymbal.

#795 Mickey Mouse Drummer. **$700.00.**
　　1938 only. Arms move, one striking drum, other the cymbal. No pie-eyes.

#795 Musical Duck. **$100.00.**
　　1952- 1954 & Easter 1955. Flip-flop feet in rhythm to musical sounds.

#798 Mickey Mouse Zilo. **$400.00.**
　　1939 – 1941. First version. Litho has hat. Five keys.
　　1942. Second version. **$400.00.**
　　Hat no longer on litho. Swinging arms and mallets striking seven keys.

#798 Chatter Monk. **$100.00.**
　　1957 – 1958. Easter 1959. Jumping motion w/swinging head. Makes chatter-chatter sound.

#799 Duckie Transport. **$400.00.**
　　1937 only. Baby ducks bounce up and down, make quack sound. Mother duck pulls ducklings in cart.

#799 Quacky Family. **$125.00.**
　　1940 – 1942. Rubber connectors allowed changing order of ducklings. Mama duck makes quack-quack sound and waddles, pulling her ducklings.

#799 Quacky Family. **$75.00.**
　　1946 – 1947 & Easter 1958. Wood dowels and felt beaks.

#799 Quacky Family. **$85.00.**
　　1948 only. Metal connectors and felt beaks.

#799 Quacky Family. **$70.00.**

1949 – 1953 & Easter 1954. Plastic beaks, metal connectors, flat hat, makes quack-quack sound.

#799 Quacky Family. **$40.00.**
　　1954 – 1958. Metal connectors, painted eyebrows and bump on hat, makes quack-quack sound.

#800 Hot Diggety. **$800.00.**
　　1934 only. Wind up to make him tap dance, pivot, pirouette, buck and wing clog. Has a cloth body, hand-painted face, and heavy metal feet.

#808 Pop 'n Ring. **$85.00.**
　　1956 – 1958 & Easter 1959. Pop-ding, pop-ding, pop-ding sounds as wood balls bounce up and down. Has 20" handle.

#809 Pop 'n Ring. **$50.00.**
　　1959 – 1961. Restyled version of the #808. Pop-ding, pop-ding, pop-ding sound when struck by new acetate bouncing balls. The last change is brightly colored lithography, has 20" long wood handle.

#810 Hot Mammy. **$800.00.**
　　1934 only. Wind up to make her tap dance, pivot, pirouette, buck and wing clog. Has a cloth body, hand-painted face, and heavy metal feet.

#810 Timber Toter. **$85.00.**
　　1957 & Easter 1958. Musical steel cylinder and wooden rattle cage. Holds 30 toy timbers.

#845 Farm Truck. **$250.00.**
　　1954 – 1955. Campbell kids, driver sways side to side with brrr-brrr sound. Veggie book with cut-out vegetables.

#870 Pull-A-Tune Xylophone. **$35.00.**
　　1957 – 1969. Wood wheels, mallet, and songbook.

#875 Looky Push Car. **$50.00.**
　　1962 – 1965 & Easter 1966. Turning steering wheel with push-button horn that beep-beeps and rotating headlight eyes, brr-rummm, brr-rumm engine sound.

#900 Struttin' Donald Duck. **$650.00.**
　　1939 & Easter 1940. Extended legs with rubber feet flip-flop, swings arms. Makes quack-quack sound.

#900 Struttin' Donald Duck. **$450.00.**
　　1940 & Easter 1941. Rubber feet on wheels flip-flop and arms swing.

#900 This Little Pig. **$55.00.**
1956 – 1958 & Easter 1959. Piggies are all pink in color and oink when squeezed, last piggy makes wee-wee-wee sound.

#900 F-P Circus. **$325.00.**
1962 – 1970. Over 1,001 exciting acts. Paraphernalia for building tricks. Circus wagon with removable top, hinged doors, lower to make unloading ramp; 11 animals and figures: seal, giraffe, bear, monkey, elephant, dog, pony, camel, lion, clown, and ringmaster. Yellow, two-piece notched plastic center ring, four ladders with three connectors, four dowels, one plastic ball with square hole, one wood barrel, trapeze, and balancing board.

#902 Junior Circus. **$225.00.**
1963 – 1970. Twenty-two of the pieces from the wagon in canister. Same figures as #900, center ring, two posts, two ladders, two connectors, wood barrel, plastic ball with square hole, and trapeze.

#905 This Little Pig. **$30.00.**
1959 – 1962. Different colored piglets. Piggies oink when squeezed, last piggy makes wee-wee-wee sound.

#910 Perpetual Motion Toy Roly-Poly. **$225.00.**
1935 only. Wooden balls connected by rubber band.

#910 Timber Toter. **$45.00.**
1958 & Easter 1959. Has 32 wood blocks and rolls on musical cylinder on back and Jack and Jill in cage cylinder on front.

#910 This Little Pig. **$30.00.**
1963 – 1965 & Easter 1966. Different colored piglets, piggies oink when squeezed, last piggy makes more of a wee-wee-wee sound. Mama Pig also has wooden ball that the earlier versions did not.

#926 Concrete Mixer Truck. **$250.00.**
1959 – 1960 & Easter 1961. Rotating drum with spring-activated plunger fires wooden balls, making pop-pop-pop sound.

#932 Amusement Park. **$325.00.**
1963 – 1965. Twenty play parts in all. Six big rides, park map, chair ride, two cars, two boats, bridge/seesaw, musical merry-go-round, swing, four-piece take-apart train, six straight body wood figures, two red, two green, two red or purple, and dog.

#940 Giant Snap-Lock Beads. **$1.00 each.**
1958 only. Twenty-four beads in three shapes, round, oval, and cylinder.

#972 Fisher Price Cash Register. **$50.00.**
1960 – 1972. Three different sized wooden coins numbered 1, 2 and 3, turn crank and drawer opens and bell rings. Press keys and Three Little Pigs, Jack and Jill, Humpty Dumpty, or Big Bad Wolf pops up.

#983 Safety School Bus. **$250.00.**
This toy is the Fisher-Price Club's famous logo.
1959 only. Four 3½" removable wood and litho figures. Bus has removable wood lid. Stop sign swings out and door opens, eyes move, and driver looks side to side. Rear two figures are permanent, bounce up and down and turn. Cool engine sound.
1960 & Easter 1961. Bus now features six 2½" removable figures.
　　Note: Author has only seen one of these buses with litho eyes instead of movable ones. No other information is available.

#984 Safety School Bus. **$225.00.**
1961 & Easter 1962. Driver eyes are litho and look left and right as bus rolls along with putt-putt-putt sound. Five wood figures, spring-hinged door, and stop sign that swings out.

#990 Safety School Bus. **$225.00.**
1962 – 1964 & Easter 1965. Driver bounces and turns as eyes on bus roll. Putt-putt sound. Spring-hinged door and swing-out stop sign, seven all-wood figures.

#997 Musical Tick-Tock Clock. **$40.00.**
1962 – 1963. Swiss music box plays "Grandfather's Clock" tune with tick-tock sound. Movable hands for teaching time. This version has a dark brown woodgrain litho with a light blue sky as the background. The sun dial also has a light blue background.
1964 – 1967. **$40.00.**
　　The only changes in this version are the much lighter brown litho and removal of light blue sky. The sundial also was changed to a dark blue on the sun side of the dial and a darker blue on the moon side.

#999 Huffy Puffy Train. **$80.00**
   1958 – 1962 Engine chug-chugs as eyes roll up and down. Coal and cattle cars and caboose with brake man swinging a lantern.
   1963 – 1970. **$45.00.**
      With railroad car.

Step Plan Block Set, also called Educational Blocks. There were many different size sets of these block sets from the early 1930s through the 1970s. This is just a small sampling of them.

#1002 Step Plan Block Set. **N/A.**
   1937 – 1941. Step 1 set. Set of 18 blocks: 12 squares and six units. See **#4005** and **#4011** for sizes of blocks.

#1002 Step Plan Block Set. **N/A.**
   1942 – 1956. Step 1 set. Seventeen blocks, five units, eight squares, two small cylinders, two round arches, and a half circle.

#1004 Fisher-Price Barrow Blocks. Step 1 toy. **N/A.**
   1933. Step 1 has 18 blocks, same as #1002 block set, and a wheelbarrow.

#1005 Push Cone. **$400.00.**
   1937 – 1938. Large six-color push toy. 18" push stick with cap that unscrews. 1¾" thick disks in various diameters slip over core, two each, red, yellow, blue, green, orange, and purple.

#1006 Floor Train. **$600.00.**
   1934 – 1938. Related in size to Fisher-Price Blocks. Blue engine, green gondola car, yellow tank car, and red caboose, 31" long.

#1007 Puzzle Barges **N/A.**
   1934. Have no other information on this toy.

#1010 Nursery Blocks, plain. **N/A.**
   1934. Have no other information on this toy.

#1012 Step 1 Blocks, colored. **N/A.**
   1933. Same as #1002 blocks, but painted.

#1014 Step 1 Colored Blocks. **N/A.**
   1934. Same as #1002 in six true non-toxic colors.

#1050 Giant Beads. **$450.00.**
   1937 – 1938. 12" peg mounted on a 4" round base. Six different shaped beads, two each red, blue, and yellow. 30" rope with ends bound in wood.

#1052 Building Peg Board. **N/A.**
   1937 – 1938. 8" x 11" board, six pegs 4½" long, 17 blocks colored red, yellow, and blue.

#1054 Color Blocks or Boxes. **$800.00.**
   1934 only. Six painted round wooden hollow tubes with caps and round balls.

#2001 Fisher-Price Coaster Blocks. **N/A.**
   1933. Rectangular wagon with wheels and rope connected to front corners of the wagon with 32 blocks: six square, eight units, four double units, two quadruple units, two pillars, two small cylinders, four large cylinders, two smalll triangles, two large triangles. Wagon is 6¼" x 12⅞" x 23⅝".

#2002 Step Plan Block Set. **N/A.**
   1937 – 1941. Step 2 set. Fourteen blocks: four units, four quadruple units, four double units, and two cylinders. See #4001 – #4003, #4005 and #4006, for block sizes.
   1942 – 1956. Twenty-seven blocks: six units, four squares, four large triangles, two round arches, three double units, two pillars, two small cylinders, two large cylinders, and a half circle.

#3002 Step Plan Block Set. **N/A.**
   1937 – 1941. Step 3 set. Twenty-eight blocks: four units, two pillars, two small cylinders, two large cylinders, eight small triangles, four large triangles, and four curves.
   1942 – 1956 Twenty-six blocks: four units, two double units, four curves, two pillars, two small cylinders, two large cylinders, eight small triangles, and two double ramps.

#4000 Fisher-Price Plain Blocks. **N/A.**
   1937 – 1954. Square. 2¾" x 2¾".

#4001 Fisher-Price Plain Blocks. **N/A.**
   1937 – 1938. Unit 1⅜" x 2¾" x 5½".

#4002 Fisher-Price Plain Blocks. **N/A.**
   1937 – 1938. Double unit 1⅜" x 2¾" x 11".

#4003 Fisher-Price Plain Blocks. **N/A.**
   1937 – 1938. Quadruple unit 1⅜" x 2¾" x 22".

#4004 Fisher-Price Plain Blocks. **N/A.**
1937 – 1938. Pillar 1⅜" x 1⅜" x 5½".

#4005 Fisher-Price Plain Blocks. **N/A.**
1937 – 1938. Small cylinder 1⅜" x 5½".

#4006 Fisher-Price Plain Blocks. **N/A.**
1937 – 1938. Large cylinder 2⅜" x 5½".

#4007 Fisher-Price Plain Blocks. **N/A.**
1937 – 1938. Small triangle 2¾" x 2¾" x 1⅜".

#4008 Fisher-Price Plain Blocks. **N/A.**
1937 – 1938. Large triangle 1⅜" x 2¾" x 5½".

#4009 Fisher-Price Plain Blocks. **N/A.**
1937 – 1938. Curve 1⅜" x 2¾" x 10".

#4010 Fisher-Price Plain Blocks. **N/A.**
1953. Round arch, half circle. 1⅜" x 2¾" x 5½".

#4011 Fisher-Price Plain Blocks. **N/A.**
1953. Double ramp 1⅜" x 2¾" x 11".

#6001 Dandy Dobbin Stick Horse. **$600.00.**
1936 only. Dandy has head of #237 and two-part 35" stick with wheels on one end.

INDEX
1964 - 1990

Each category is listed alphabetically and the toys are then listed alphabetically within the categories. I have listed the toys by name, followed by the toy number, and page number. Most of the time Fisher-Price has the name of the toy on it. Using the toy number, go to it in the book for a detailed description and value. All the toys in the front are in numerical order.

Husky Sets

Little People Play Sets

Music Box Radios, TVs, and Toys

Puzzles

THE FISHER-PRICE COLLECTORS CLUB

The Fisher-Price Collectors Club is a rapidly expanding non-profit club organized for the caring and sharing of Fisher-Price toys. We were organized in 1993 and incorporated in Arizona in 1994. We received notification from the Internal Revenue Service that effective since 1994, **The Fisher-Price Collectors Club** is recognized as a not-for-profit company under the Internal Revenue Code section 501(c)(3). As such, contributions made to the Fisher-Price Collectors Club are deductible as charitable contributions. Membership fees are not charitable contributions. Members elect the Board of Directors. The purpose of the corporation is to study, research, discuss, and write about Fisher-Price toys; to preserve and promote the collection of Fisher-Price toys and related items; and to contribute to those activities for which the purposes are charitable, scientific, literary, or educational. The club holds an annual convention in conjunction with ToyFest in August, in East Aurora, NY, home of Fisher-Price. *The Gabby Goose* newsletter is published quarterly by the club. Material and ads must be submitted one month before the issue dates of March, June, September, and December. Ads are free to members, up to 40 words.

We cordially invite you to join this special toy club. As a member, you will meet the many toy collectors who have already joined our club, exchanging information and sharing experiences about collecting Fisher-Price toys through *The Gabby Goose* newsletter. To become a member, simply fill out the form below and include your check for $20.00, payable to FPCC, for a one-year membership. (The year runs from September to August. Dues are not pro-rated; when you join, you receive all prior newsletters for that year.)

Mail this form and your check to Jeanne Kennedy, 1442 North Ogden, Mesa, AZ 83205

Name _____ Phone _____

Address _____

City _____ State _____ Zip _____

COLLECTOR BOOKS

Informing Today's Collector

For over two decades we have been keeping collectors informed on trends and values in all fields of antiques and collectibles.

DOLLS, FIGURES & TEDDY BEARS

4707	A Decade of **Barbie** Dolls & Collectibles, 1981–1991, Summers	$19.95
4631	**Barbie** Doll Boom, 1986–1995, Augustyniak	$18.95
2079	**Barbie** Doll Fashion, Volume I, Eames	$24.95
4846	**Barbie** Doll Fashion, Volume II, Eames	$24.95
3957	**Barbie** Exclusives, Rana	$18.95
4632	**Barbie** Exclusives, Book II, Rana	$18.95
4557	**Barbie**, The First 30 Years, Deutsch	$24.95
4847	**Barbie** Years, 1959–1995, 2nd Ed., Olds	$17.95
3310	**Black Dolls**, 1820–1991, Perkins	$17.95
3873	**Black Dolls**, Book II, Perkins	$17.95
3810	**Chatty Cathy Dolls**, Lewis	$15.95
1529	Collector's Encyclopedia of **Barbie** Dolls, DeWein	$19.95
4882	Collector's Encyclopedia of **Barbie** Doll Exclusives and More, Augustyniak	$19.95
2211	Collector's Encyclopedia of **Madame Alexander Dolls**, Smith	$24.95
4863	Collector's Encyclopedia of **Vogue Dolls**, Izen/Stover	$29.95
3967	Collector's Guide to **Trolls**, Peterson	$19.95
4571	**Liddle Kiddles**, Identification & Value Guide, Langford	$18.95
3826	Story of **Barbie**, Westenhouser	$19.95
1513	**Teddy Bears & Steiff** Animals, Mandel	$9.95
1817	**Teddy Bears & Steiff** Animals, 2nd Series, Mandel	$19.95
2084	**Teddy Bears, Annalee's & Steiff** Animals, 3rd Series, Mandel	$19.95
1808	Wonder of **Barbie**, Manos	$9.95
1430	World of **Barbie** Dolls, Manos	$9.95
4880	World of **Raggedy Ann** Collectibles, Avery	$24.95

TOYS, MARBLES & CHRISTMAS COLLECTIBLES

3427	**Advertising Character** Collectibles, Dotz	$17.95
2333	Antique & Collector's **Marbles**, 3rd Ed., Grist	$9.95
3827	Antique & Collector's **Toys**, 1870–1950, Longest	$24.95
3956	Baby Boomer **Games**, Identification & Value Guide, Polizzi	$24.95
4934	**Breyer Animal** Collector's Guide, Identification and Values, Browell	$19.95
3717	**Christmas** Collectibles, 2nd Edition, Whitmyer	$24.95
4976	**Christmas** Ornaments, Lights & Decorations, Johnson	$24.95
4737	**Christmas** Ornaments, Lights & Decorations, Vol. II, Johnson	$24.95
4739	**Christmas** Ornaments, Lights & Decorations, Vol. III, Johnson	$24.95
4649	Classic Plastic **Model Kits**, Polizzi	$24.95
4559	Collectible **Action Figures**, 2nd Ed., Manos	$17.95
3874	Collectible Coca-Cola Toy **Trucks**, deCourtivron	$24.95
2338	Collector's Encyclopedia of **Disneyana**, Longest, Stern	$24.95
4958	Collector's Guide to **Battery Toys**, Hultzman	$19.95
4639	Collector's Guide to **Diecast Toys & Scale Models**, Johnson	$19.95
4651	Collector's Guide to **Tinker Toys**, Strange	$18.95
4566	Collector's Guide to **Tootsietoys**, 2nd Ed., Richter	$19.95
4720	The Golden Age of **Automotive Toys**, 1925–1941, Hutchison/Johnson	$24.95
3436	Grist's Big Book of **Marbles**	$19.95
3970	Grist's Machine-Made & Contemporary **Marbles**, 2nd Ed.	$9.95
4723	**Matchbox** Toys, 1947 to 1996, 2nd Ed., Johnson	$18.95
4871	**McDonald's Collectibles**, Henriques/DuVall	$19.95
1540	**Modern Toys** 1930–1980, Baker	$19.95
3888	**Motorcycle** Toys, Antique & Contemporary, Gentry/Downs	$18.95
4953	Schroeder's Collectible **Toys**, Antique to Modern Price Guide, 4th Ed.	$17.95
1886	Stern's Guide to **Disney** Collectibles	$14.95
2139	Stern's Guide to **Disney** Collectibles, 2nd Series	$14.95
3975	Stern's Guide to **Disney** Collectibles, 3rd Series	$18.95
2028	**Toys**, Antique & Collectible, Longest	$14.95
3979	**Zany Characters** of the Ad World, Lamphier	$16.95

FURNITURE

1457	American **Oak** Furniture, McNerney	$9.95
3716	American **Oak** Furniture, Book II, McNerney	$12.95
1118	Antique **Oak** Furniture, Hill	$7.95
2271	Collector's Encyclopedia of **American** Furniture, Vol. II, Swedberg	$24.95
3720	Collector's Encyclopedia of **American** Furniture, Vol. III, Swedberg	$24.95
3878	Collector's Guide to **Oak** Furniture, George	$12.95
1755	Furniture of the **Depression Era**, Swedberg	$19.95
3906	**Heywood-Wakefield** Modern Furniture, Rouland	$18.95

1885	**Victorian** Furniture, Our American Heritage, McNerney	$9.95
3829	**Victorian** Furniture, Our American Heritage, Book II, McNerney	$9.95

JEWELRY, HATPINS, WATCHES & PURSES

1712	Antique & Collector's **Thimbles** & Accessories, Mathis	$19.95
1748	Antique **Purses**, Revised Second Ed., Holiner	$19.95
1278	Art Nouveau & Art Deco **Jewelry**, Baker	$9.95
4850	Collectible **Costume Jewelry**, Simonds	$24.95
3875	Collecting Antique **Stickpins**, Kerins	$16.95
3722	Collector's Ency. of **Compacts, Carryalls & Face Powder Boxes**, Mueller	$24.95
4854	Collector's Ency. of **Compacts, Carryalls & Face Powder Boxes**, Vol. II	$24.95
4940	**Costume Jewelry**, A Practical Handbook & Value Guide, Rezazadeh	$24.95
1716	Fifty Years of Collectible **Fashion Jewelry**, 1925–1975, Baker	$19.95
1424	**Hatpins** & Hatpin Holders, Baker	$9.95
4570	Ladies' **Compacts**, Gerson	$24.95
1181	100 Years of Collectible **Jewelry**, 1850–1950, Baker	$9.95
4729	**Sewing Tools** & Trinkets, Thompson	$24.95
2348	20th Century Fashionable Plastic **Jewelry**, Baker	$19.95
4878	Vintage & Contemporary **Purse Accessories**, Gerson	$24.95
3830	Vintage **Vanity Bags & Purses**, Gerson	$24.95

INDIANS, GUNS, KNIVES, TOOLS, PRIMITIVES

1868	Antique **Tools**, Our American Heritage, McNerney	$9.95
1426	**Arrowheads** & Projectile Points, Hothem	$7.95
4943	Field Guide to **Flint Arrowheads & Knives** of the North American Indian	$9.95
2279	**Indian Artifacts** of the Midwest, Hothem	$14.95
3885	**Indian Artifacts** of the Midwest, Book II, Hothem	$16.95
4870	**Indian Artifacts** of the Midwest, Book III, Hothem	$18.95
1964	**Indian Axes** & Related Stone Artifacts, Hothem	$14.95
2023	**Keen Kutter** Collectibles, Heuring	$14.95
4724	Modern **Guns**, Identification & Values, 11th Ed., Quertermous	$12.95
2164	**Primitives**, Our American Heritage, McNerney	$9.95
1759	**Primitives**, Our American Heritage, 2nd Series, McNerney	$14.95
4730	Standard **Knife** Collector's Guide, 3rd Ed., Ritchie & Stewart	$12.95

PAPER COLLECTIBLES & BOOKS

4633	**Big Little Books**, Jacobs	$18.95
4710	Collector's Guide to **Children's Books**, Jones	$18.95
1441	Collector's Guide to **Post Cards**, Wood	$9.95
2081	Guide to Collecting **Cookbooks**, Allen	$14.95
2080	Price Guide to **Cookbooks & Recipe Leaflets**, Dickinson	$9.95
3973	**Sheet Music** Reference & Price Guide, 2nd Ed., Pafik & Guiheen	$19.95
4654	**Victorian Trade Cards**, Historical Reference & Value Guide, Cheadle	$19.95
4733	**Whitman Juvenile Books**, Brown	$17.95

GLASSWARE

4561	Collectible **Drinking Glasses**, Chase & Kelly	$17.95
4642	Collectible **Glass Shoes**, Wheatley	$19.95
4937	Coll. **Glassware from the 40s, 50s & 60s**, 4th Ed., Florence	$19.95
1810	Collector's Encyclopedia of **American Art Glass**, Shuman	$29.95
4938	Collector's Encyclopedia of **Depression Glass**, 13th Ed., Florence	$19.95
1961	Collector's Encyclopedia of **Fry Glassware**, Fry Glass Society	$24.95
1664	Collector's Encyclopedia of **Heisey Glass**, 1925–1938, Bredehoft	$24.95
3905	Collector's Encyclopedia of **Milk Glass**, Newbound	$24.95
4936	Collector's Guide to **Candy Containers**, Dezso/Poirier	$19.95
4564	**Crackle Glass**, Weitman	$19.95
4941	**Crackle Glass**, Book II, Weitman	$19.95
2275	**Czechoslovakian Glass** and Collectibles, Barta/Rose	$16.95
4714	**Czechoslovakian Glass** and Collectibles, Book II, Barta/Rose	$16.95
4716	**Elegant Glassware** of the Depression Era, 7th Ed., Florence	$19.95
1380	Encyclopedia of **Pattern Glass**, McClain	$12.95
3981	Ever's Standard **Cut Glass** Value Guide	$12.95
4659	**Fenton** Art Glass, 1907–1939, Whitmyer	$24.95
3725	**Fostoria**, Pressed, Blown & Hand Molded Shapes, Kerr	$24.95
4719	**Fostoria**, Etched, Carved & Cut Designs, Vol. II, Kerr	$24.95
3883	**Fostoria Stemware**, The Crystal for America, Long & Seate	$24.95
4644	**Imperial Carnival Glass**, Burns	$18.95
3886	**Kitchen Glassware** of the Depression Years, 5th Ed., Florence	$19.95

COLLECTOR BOOKS
Informing Today's Collector

4725	Pocket Guide to **Depression Glass**, 10th Ed., Florence	$9.95
5035	Standard Encyclopedia of **Carnival Glass**, 6th Ed., Edwards/Carwile	$24.95
5036	Standard **Carnival Glass** Price Guide, 11th Ed., Edwards/Carwile	$9.95
4875	Standard Encyclopedia of **Opalescent Glass**, 2nd ed., Edwards	$19.95
4731	**Stemware Identification**, Featuring Cordials with Values, Florence	$24.95
3326	**Very Rare Glassware** of the Depression Years, 3rd Series, Florence	$24.95
4732	**Very Rare Glassware** of the Depression Years, 5th Series, Florence	$24.95
4656	**Westmoreland Glass**, Wilson	$24.95

POTTERY

4927	**ABC Plates & Mugs**, Lindsay	$24.95
4929	**American Art Pottery**, Sigafoose	$24.95
4630	**American Limoges**, Limoges	$24.95
1312	**Blue & White Stoneware**, McNerney	$9.95
1958	So. Potteries **Blue Ridge Dinnerware**, 3rd Ed., Newbound	$14.95
1959	**Blue Willow**, 2nd Ed., Gaston	$14.95
4848	Ceramic **Coin Banks**, Stoddard	$19.95
4851	Collectible **Cups & Saucers**, Harran	$18.95
4709	Collectible **Kay Finch**, Biography, Identification & Values, Martinez/Frick	$18.95
1373	Collector's Encyclopedia of **American Dinnerware**, Cunningham	$24.95
4931	Collector's Encyclopedia of **Bauer Pottery**, Chipman	$24.95
3815	Collector's Encyclopedia of **Blue Ridge Dinnerware**, Newbound	$19.95
4932	Collector's Encyclopedia of **Blue Ridge Dinnerware**, Vol. II, Newbound	$24.95
4658	Collector's Encyclopedia of **Brush-McCoy Pottery**, Huxford	$24.95
2272	Collector's Encyclopedia of **California Pottery**, Chipman	$24.95
3811	Collector's Encyclopedia of **Colorado Pottery**, Carlton	$24.95
2133	Collector's Encyclopedia of **Cookie Jars**, Roerig	$24.95
3723	Collector's Encyclopedia of **Cookie Jars**, Book II, Roerig	$24.95
4939	Collector's Encyclopedia of **Cookie Jars**, Book III, Roerig	$24.95
4638	Collector's Encyclopedia of **Dakota Potteries**, Dommel	$24.95
5040	Collector's Encyclopedia of **Fiesta**, 8th Ed., Huxford	$19.95
4718	Collector's Encyclopedia of **Figural Planters & Vases**, Newbound	$19.95
3961	Collector's Encyclopedia of **Early Noritake**, Alden	$24.95
1439	Collector's Encyclopedia of **Flow Blue China**, Gaston	$19.95
3812	Collector's Encyclopedia of **Flow Blue China**, 2nd Ed., Gaston	$24.95
3813	Collector's Encyclopedia of **Hall China**, 2nd Ed., Whitmyer	$24.95
3431	Collector's Encyclopedia of **Homer Laughlin China**, Jasper	$24.95
1276	Collector's Encyclopedia of **Hull Pottery**, Roberts	$19.95
3962	Collector's Encyclopedia of **Lefton China**, DeLozier	$19.95
4855	Collector's Encyclopedia of **Lefton China**, Book II, DeLozier	$19.95
2210	Collector's Encyclopedia of **Limoges Porcelain**, 2nd Ed., Gaston	$24.95
2334	Collector's Encyclopedia of **Majolica Pottery**, Katz-Marks	$19.95
1358	Collector's Encyclopedia of **McCoy Pottery**, Huxford	$19.95
3963	Collector's Encyclopedia of **Metlox Potteries**, Gibbs Jr.	$24.95
3837	Collector's Encyclopedia of **Nippon Porcelain**, Van Patten	$24.95
2089	Collector's Ency. of **Nippon Porcelain**, 2nd Series, Van Patten	$24.95
1665	Collector's Ency. of **Nippon Porcelain**, 3rd Series, Van Patten	$24.95
4712	Collector's Ency. of **Nippon Porcelain**, 4th Series, Van Patten	$24.95
1447	Collector's Encyclopedia of **Noritake**, Van Patten	$19.95
3432	Collector's Encyclopedia of **Noritake**, 2nd Series, Van Patten	$24.95
1037	Collector's Encyclopedia of **Occupied Japan**, 1st Series, Florence	$14.95
1038	Collector's Encyclopedia of **Occupied Japan**, 2nd Series, Florence	$14.95
2088	Collector's Encyclopedia of **Occupied Japan**, 3rd Series, Florence	$14.95
2019	Collector's Encyclopedia of **Occupied Japan**, 4th Series, Florence	$14.95
2335	Collector's Encyclopedia of **Occupied Japan**, 5th Series, Florence	$14.95
4951	Collector's Encyclopedia of **Old Ivory China**, Hillman	$24.95
3964	Collector's Encyclopedia of **Pickard China**, Reed	$24.95
3877	Collector's Encyclopedia of **R.S. Prussia**, 4th Series, Gaston	$24.95
1034	Collector's Encyclopedia of **Roseville Pottery**, Huxford	$19.95
1035	Collector's Encyclopedia of **Roseville Pottery**, 2nd Ed., Huxford	$19.95
4856	Collector's Encyclopeida of **Russel Wright**, 2nd Ed., Kerr	$24.95
4713	Collector's Encyclopedia of **Salt Glaze Stoneware**, Taylor/Lowrance	$24.95
3314	Collector's Encyclopedia of **Van Briggle Art Pottery**, Sasicki	$24.95
4563	Collector's Encyclopedia of **Wall Pockets**, Newbound	$19.95
2111	Collector's Encyclopedia of **Weller Pottery**, Huxford	$29.95
3876	Collector's Guide to **Lu-Ray Pastels**, Meehan	$18.95
3814	Collector's Guide to **Made in Japan** Ceramics, White	$18.95
4646	Collector's Guide to **Made in Japan** Ceramics, Book II, White	$18.95
4565	Collector's Guide to **Rockingham**, The Enduring Ware, Brewer	$14.95
2339	Collector's Guide to **Shawnee Pottery**, Vanderbilt	$19.95
1425	**Cookie Jars**, Westfall	$9.95

3440	**Cookie Jars**, Book II, Westfall	$19.95
4924	Figural & Novelty **Salt & Pepper Shakers**, 2nd Series, Davern	$24.95
2379	Lehner's Ency. of **U.S. Marks** on Pottery, Porcelain & China	$24.95
4722	**McCoy Pottery**, Collector's Reference & Value Guide, Hanson/Nissen	$19.95
3825	**Purinton Pottery**, Morris	$24.95
4726	**Red Wing Art Pottery**, 1920s–1960s, Dollen	$19.95
1670	**Red Wing Collectibles**, DePasquale	$9.95
1440	**Red Wing Stoneware**, DePasquale	$9.95
1632	**Salt & Pepper Shakers**, Guarnaccia	$9.95
5091	**Salt & Pepper Shakers** II, Guarnaccia	$18.95
2220	**Salt & Pepper Shakers** III, Guarnaccia	$14.95
3443	**Salt & Pepper Shakers** IV, Guarnaccia	$18.95
3738	**Shawnee Pottery**, Mangus	$24.95
4629	Turn of the Century **American Dinnerware**, 1880s–1920s, Jasper	$24.95
4572	**Wall Pockets** of the Past, Perkins	$17.95
3327	**Watt Pottery** – Identification & Value Guide, Morris	$19.95

OTHER COLLECTIBLES

4704	Antique & Collectible **Buttons**, Wisniewski	$19.95
2269	Antique **Brass & Copper** Collectibles, Gaston	$16.95
1880	Antique **Iron**, McNerney	$9.95
3872	Antique **Tins**, Dodge	$24.95
4845	Antique **Typewriters & Office Collectibles**, Rehr	$19.95
1714	**Black** Collectibles, Gibbs	$19.95
1128	**Bottle** Pricing Guide, 3rd Ed., Cleveland	$7.95
4636	**Celluloid Collectibles**, Dunn	$14.95
3718	Collectible **Aluminum**, Grist	$16.95
3445	Collectible **Cats**, An Identification & Value Guide, Fyke	$18.95
4560	Collectible **Cats**, An Identification & Value Guide, Book II, Fyke	$19.95
4852	Collectible **Compact Disc** Price Guide 2, Cooper	$17.95
2018	Collector's Encyclopedia of **Granite Ware**, Greguire	$24.95
3430	Collector's Encyclopedia of **Granite Ware**, Book 2, Greguire	$24.95
4705	Collector's Guide to **Antique Radios**, 4th Ed., Bunis	$18.95
3880	Collector's Guide to **Cigarette Lighters**, Flanagan	$17.95
4637	Collector's Guide to **Cigarette Lighers**, Book II, Flanagan	$17.95
4942	Collector's Guide to **Don Winton Designs**, Ellis	$19.95
3966	Collector's Guide to **Inkwells**, Identification & Values, Badders	$18.95
4947	Collector's Guide to **Inkwells**, Book II, Badders	$19.95
4948	Collector's Guide to **Letter Openers**, Grist	$19.95
4862	Collector's Guide to **Toasters** & Accessories, Greguire	$19.95
4652	Collector's Guide to **Transistor Radios**, 2nd Ed., Bunis	$16.95
4653	Collector's Guide to **TV Memorabilia**, 1960s–1970s, Davis/Morgan	$24.95
4864	Collector's Guide to **Wallace Nutting Pictures**, Ivankovich	$18.95
1629	**Doorstops**, Identification & Values, Bertoia	$9.95
4567	Figural **Napkin Rings**, Gottschalk & Whitson	$18.95
4717	Figural **Nodders**, Includes Bobbin' Heads and Swayers, Irtz	$19.95
3968	**Fishing Lure** Collectibles, Murphy/Edmisten	$24.95
4867	**Flea Market Trader**, 11th Ed., Huxford	$9.95
4944	**Flue Covers**, Collector's Value Guide, Meckley	$12.95
4945	**G-Men and FBI Toys** and Collectibles, Whitworth	$18.95
5043	**Garage Sale & Flea Market Annual**, 6th Ed.	$19.95
3819	**General Store Collectibles**, Wilson	$24.95
4643	**Great American West** Collectibles, Wilson	$24.95
2215	Goldstein's **Coca-Cola** Collectibles	$16.95
3884	Huxford's Collectible **Advertising**, 2nd Ed.	$24.95
2216	**Kitchen Antiques**, 1790–1940, McNerney	$14.95
4950	The **Lone Ranger**, Collector's Reference & Value Guide, Felbinger	$18.95
2026	**Railroad** Collectibles, 4th Ed., Baker	$14.95
4949	**Schroeder's Antiques Price Guide**, 16th Ed., Huxford	$12.95
5007	**Silverplated Flatware**, Revised 4th Edition, Hagan	$18.95
1922	Standard **Old Bottle** Price Guide, Sellari	$14.95
4708	Summers' Guide to **Coca-Cola**	$19.95
4952	Summers' Pocket Guide to **Coca-Cola** Identifications	$9.95
3892	**Toy & Miniature Sewing Machines**, Thomas	$18.95
4876	**Toy & Miniature Sewing Machines**, Book II, Thomas	$24.95
3828	Value Guide to **Advertising Memorabilia**, Summers	$18.95
3977	Value Guide to **Gas Station** Memorabilia, Summers & Priddy	$24.95
4877	Vintage **Bar Ware**, Visakay	$24.95
4935	The W.F. Cody **Buffalo Bill** Collector's Guide with Values	$24.95
4879	**Wanted to Buy**, 6th Edition	$9.95

This is only a partial listing of the books on antiques that are available from Collector Books. All books are well illustrated and contain current values. Most of these books are available from your local bookseller, antique dealer, or public library. If you are unable to locate certain titles in your area, you may order by mail from COLLECTOR BOOKS, P.O. Box 3009, Paducah, KY 42002-3009. Customers with Visa, Discover or MasterCard may phone in orders from 7:00–5:00 CST, Monday–Friday, Toll Free 1-800-626-5420. Add $2.00 for postage for the first book ordered and $0.30 for each additional book. Include item number, title, and price when ordering. Allow 14 to 21 days for delivery.

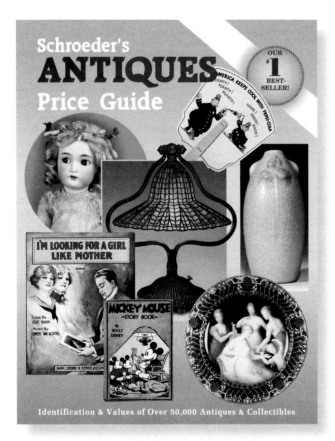